Fire Safety Law

Fire Safety Law provides building-owners, managers, individual leaseholders, mortgage-lenders, landlords, and anyone involved in the purchase or sale of a flat situated within a multi-occupied block, with practical, yet comprehensive and well-researched information regarding the subject of fire safety and the associated responsibilities, obligations and rights.

V. Charles Ward addresses in practical legal terms the responsibilities on building-owners to ensure that buildings are fire-safe for people who are living, working, or visiting those buildings and explains what protections are available to leaseholders faced with the costs of making their buildings fire-safe. The book begins with a summary of the lessons which have come from the Grenfell Inquiry, before providing a practical overview of current fire-safety legislation relating to residential and commercial buildings.

This legislative overview will include not only the 2005 Fire Safety Order, as updated by the 2021 Fire Safety Act and the Fire Safety (England) Regulations 2022, but will also include associated and emerging legislation and official guidance in relation to fire safety, including gas and electrical safety regulation, as well as the Building Safety Act 2022. The book will then pull apart a typical long-residential lease within a high-rise block to identify who is directly responsible for fire safety and explain how the costs of making good the fire-risk from defective cladding might be shared out between the ground-landlord and individual residential leaseholders.

Having assessed the legal situation as regards existing high-rise leaseholders, the book then addresses the additional 'due diligence' required by prospective purchasers of individual high-rise flats, as well as estate agents, mortgage-lenders, landlords and conveyancing lawyers, to ensure that what they will be buying or lending money on is 'fire-safe' and that any associated costs are fully accounted for.

V. Charles Ward is a solicitor and a Legal Associate of the Royal Town Planning Institute. His professional background spans private practice, industry, local government and urban regeneration projects. Since 2013, he has been working as a property lawyer with HB Public Law, a shared legal service acting for several local authorities. Other books by Charles Ward include *Residential Leaseholders' Handbook* (2006), and *Housing Regeneration: A Plan for Implementation* (2018).

Fire Safety Law
A Practical Guide for Leaseholders,
Building-Owners and Conveyancers

V. Charles Ward

LONDON AND NEW YORK

First published 2023
by Routledge
4 Park Square, Milton Park, Abingdon, Oxon OX14 4RN

and by Routledge
605 Third Avenue, New York, NY 10158

Routledge is an imprint of the Taylor & Francis Group, an informa business

© 2023 V. Charles Ward

The right of V. Charles Ward to be identified as author of this work has been asserted in accordance with sections 77 and 78 of the Copyright, Designs and Patents Act 1988.

All rights reserved. No part of this book may be reprinted or reproduced or utilised in any form or by any electronic, mechanical, or other means, now known or hereafter invented, including photocopying and recording, or in any information storage or retrieval system, without permission in writing from the publishers.

Trademark notice: Product or corporate names may be trademarks or registered trademarks, and are used only for identification and explanation without intent to infringe.

British Library Cataloguing-in-Publication Data
A catalogue record for this book is available from the British Library

Library of Congress Cataloging-in-Publication Data
A catalog record has been requested for this book

ISBN: 978-1-032-27222-1 (hbk)
ISBN: 978-1-032-27141-5 (pbk)
ISBN: 978-1-003-29189-3 (ebk)

DOI: 10.1201/9781003291893

Typeset in Times New Roman
by Taylor & Francis Books

Contents

1	The problem	1
2	The Grenfell Inquiry	8
3	The Fire Safety Order (FSO)	14
4	PAS 9980:2022 Fire Risk Appraisal of External Wall Construction and Cladding of Existing Blocks of Flats: Code of Practice	40
5	Fire safety and leasehold frameworks	49
6	The Defective Premises Act 1972 (DPA) (as amended)	67
7	Fire safety and the Building Regulations 2010 (as updated)	71
8	Building warranties and fire safety	83
9	Government assistance to remove defective cladding	87
10	Buying a flat in a high-rise block	98
11	The EWS1 form	102
12	Private landlord responsibilities relating to fire safety	107
	Index	113

1 The problem

Everyone knows that a problem exists. And that it has to be solved. The main questions are: how much will it cost? And who should pay for it? Until these questions are answered, thousands of residential leaseholders will be living in buildings which are potentially unsafe because of the type of external cladding which was used in their construction or refurbishment.

Even if there is no actual confirmed fire-risk, a second group of leaseholders may find that their flats are, for practical purposes, unmortgageable and therefore unsaleable, because of the possibility that the construction of those buildings might constitute a fire-risk, no matter how remote the actual risk of fire in that building might be.

The lives of that second group of leaseholders are also on hold until it can be confirmed, through testing, that the external wall system used in the construction or refurbishment of their flats is 100 per cent safe. For a number of reasons, that testing process itself can be slow and expensive.

The victims of the Grenfell Tower block fire of 14 June 2017 were not just the 72 people who lost their lives. Nor just the immediate families of those people. Nor the additional 70 (plus) people who suffered injury from the fire. Counted amongst the victims must be every residential leaseholder living in a similar tower block with similar external cladding systems. For every residential leaseholder in any of those blocks, Grenfell is a personal disaster. It's not just that they are living within a potential fire-risk, until defective cladding is removed. There is also the sensitive question of who pays for it? Is it the government? Is it the building-owner? Should liability be passed back to whoever originally installed the defective cladding, no matter how long ago? Or is the cost of replacing defective cladding something which will inevitably be passed back to individual leaseholders and paid through service charges?

It will be a lucky leaseholder who is not asked to bear at least part of that cost. Many of those leaseholders will also be in negative equity. That is to say that they have mortgage liabilities worth more than the residual value of their flats. It means that even if they gave away their flats for nothing, they still face a large unsecured mortgage debt. Who is going to pay that if they are declared bankrupt?

Reputedly worst hit are leaseholders in Manchester's Connect House, some of whom are facing bills of up to £115,000 each to cover the £5.2 million cost

DOI: 10.1201/9781003291893-1

of removing Grenfell-style cladding, with an average leaseholder bill of £78,000. Connect House is a building which was converted into flats and commercial space as recently as 2003 in compliance with planning laws and building regulations in force at that time. Following a comprehensive risk assessment carried out in March 2020, the building was found to be unsafe. Leaseholders could be responsible for up to 70 per cent of the cost of putting right the defects.

In May 2021, four years after Grenfell, there was a second tower block fire involving defective cladding at New Providence Wharf, Poplar, East London. It reminds us that Grenfell was not just a tragic one-off but that the continuing risk of fire from defective cladding is real. Fortunately, in the New Providence incident, no one was killed. Was this because residents were already alert to the problem and the need to vacate the building immediately in the event of fire?

Residents, as well as building-owner Ballymore, had previously identified a cladding issue relating to the building and works to remove the defective cladding were scheduled to start. In the meantime a 'waking watch' had been put in place to alert residents if a fire took place. Was it also fortuitous that the New Providence Wharf fire started at 9 a.m. in the morning when most residents were already awake?

The cost of fixing defective cladding at New Providence Wharf had been estimated at £11.6 million, of which Ballymore, as the building-owner, would contribute £500,000 and with leaseholders facing a combined bill of £3.1 million.

There is also a mutual interest in getting cladding issues fixed sooner rather than later. It is not just about removing an on-going fire-risk. If a programme of remediation is not put in hand, leaseholders may still face the interim on-going cost of a waking watch, which involves employing security personnel to patrol the building 24/7 to look out for signs of fire and alert residents.

The Ministry of Housing, Communities and Local Government (MHCLG) research and analysis document, 'Building Safety Programme: Waking Watch Costs', refers to a monthly mean waking watch cost of £17,897 across England, rising to £20,443 in London. For individual leaseholders, that monthly cost translates to £331 per flat, rising to £499 in London. Couldn't that money be better spent?

Whilst the government has introduced a £30,000,000 'Waking Watch Relief Fund', the purpose of that fund is not to subsidise the on-going cost of employing a waking watch but instead to fund the cost of fire-alarm systems to replace the need for a waking watch.

Apart from the costs of a waking watch, leaseholders in buildings with an identified fire-risk are also likely to face increased insurance costs. If they can get insurance at all.

Fire-risk in a high-rise block, or for that matter any other multi-occupied residential building, is not just about flammable cladding. Although it is the dangers from flammable cladding identified as a result of the 2017 Grenfell disaster which are now driving the fire-risk agenda, at least as regards multi-storey apartments and not just those rising more than 18 metres. It is why this book focuses on the law relating to fire-risk in multi-occupied residential buildings. It is also why the type of flammable aluminium composite material used in Grenfell has to be a starting point for this book.

It is that issue which is most financially threatening to residential leaseholders. It is that issue which is currently driving the government's legislative agenda on matters relating to fire-risk. It is that issue which has become the new work stream for the First Tier Tribunal, which has to arbitrate on such issues between ground-landlords, management companies and leaseholders.

The term 'cladding' in this context refers to the components attached to the primary structure of a building to form non-structural external services, as opposed to buildings in which the external services are formed by structural elements, such as masonry walls. Aluminium composite material (ACM) parts had been used as a form of rainscreen cladding as part of a double-wall construction. Rainscreen prevents water ingress into the wall construction. Thermal insulation, air tightness and structural stability are provided by the second inner part of the wall construction. With ACM, two screens of aluminium are bonded to either side of a lightweight core of materials, such as polyethylene or a mineral core. During a fire, the parts can delaminate and expose the core material.

In the Grenfell block, the more flammable Reynobond PE polyethylene core was used instead of the fire-resistant Reynobond FR core. Though at the time of the Grenfell fire, Reynobond PE was not banned in the UK.

Although the use of ACM cladding in an external wall system can create a fire hazard, it is not the only possible cause, as is apparent from the Probyn Miers Report into the fire at Richmond House, Worcester Park, London KT4, which happened in the morning of Monday, 9 September 2019. That fire spread rapidly and destroyed much of the block despite the efforts of 125 firefighters who arrived within 9 minutes of receiving the alarm. The Probyn Miers Report considers the construction of the building and why the fire was able to spread so rapidly in its early stages.

The internal walls of that building were constructed of plasterboard attached to timber stud walls, typically with two layers bonded to each side. This recognised and long-established provision of fire-protection is effective and reliable so long as the boarding is continuous and properly attached to the studs and any gaps or penetrations around cables or pipes are sealed using fire-resistant materials. The effectiveness of fire-protection in internal walls also depends on any doors in those walls being fire-doors which provide an appropriate level of protection.

From drawings contained within the Richmond House report, it is clear that the internal walls and doors resisted the spread of fire more effectively than the external walls. While the flats to the south-west of the circulation corridor were almost completely destroyed, those to the north-east suffered little direct damage from the fire. Those parts of the building were damaged

4   *The problem*

by smoke and by firefighting water and the instability in the structure as a whole. But the fire was held back in those parts of the building for a reasonable period of time.

The report also highlights the contrast in the building between those parts which were badly damaged and those which were not. The escape staircase, which was constructed to provide protection for those escaping from the building, remained largely undamaged. But the framework was finished externally in glass-reinforced plastic.

The Richmond House building was largely timber-framed with elements of structural steelwork, built over the concrete-framed basement. The external walls were finished in a cement board material called Hardie Plank, manufactured by James Hardie Building Products Limited, which, in the Standard Fire Classification, achieves a rating of A2, s1-d0. This means that the material is of 'limited combustibility'. On exposure to fire, it does not flame and contribute to the development of the fire.

A2 describes a high standard of fire resistance. Other materials classified as A2 include plasterboard and some types of mineral wall. The higher A1 classification applies entirely to non-combustible materials, such as concrete, glass or cast iron. It is the highest classification in terms of smoke production, meaning that on exposure to fire, it produces little or no smoke. Nor does it produce burning droplets.

In Richmond House, the Hardie Plank was fixed to three layers of timber battens of varying thicknesses which held the Hardie Plank away from the main timber structure. These battens created a void approximately 16 centimetres deep between the boarding and the main structure to the full height of the building. Once the fire entered this void, it was able to spread very quickly around the outside of the building, as the battens, being of natural timber, burned easily. The spread of fire behind the cladding should have been slowed substantially by 'cavity barriers' which should have been fitted within the void created by the battens around all window and door openings in the external wall; on the floor lines; and on party wall lines. Cavity barriers are most often formed of blocks of dense mineral wall insulation in a polythene sleeve. But to be effective, they have to be compressed in position and to fully close the cavity.

Cavity barriers do not completely prevent the spread of fire, but slow it enough so that firefighters can tackle it within a limited area. In Richmond House, the cavity barriers which were fitted were found to be defective because they were too small to close the cavity and they would have contributed nothing to control the fire. These defects in cavity barrier installation appeared to have been the result of design errors.

The external balcony at Richmond House had a steel structure but the framework was finished externally in glass-reinforced plastic (GRP) and the deck was formed in natural timber. Both the GRP and timber burn readily and both contributed to the development of the fire on the south-west elevation. In some places that the fire did not reach, the heat was such that the

GRP softened and slumped. Because effective cavity barriers were not fitted in the external wall void, in its early stages, the fire was able to spread almost unhindered both horizontally and vertically.

When it reached the roof, there was no effective obstacle preventing fire spreading to the roof, which there should have been. Fire also spread along the eaves, at the base of the roof. The eaves were boxed in using a dense plastic board, which burned readily and melted away. This board was fixed to timber battens held off the main wall of the building. Again, cavity barriers should have been installed in the boxing of the eaves to prevent the spread of the fire. But these were absent.

The roof itself was finished with slate fixed to timber battens, with a waterproof membrane underneath. The roof structure was timber. Fire-stopping should have been present under the slates, on the lines of the party walls, but it may have been absent because the spread of fire across the roof did not appear to have been delayed on the party wall lines. Though if this fire-stopping was absent, that defect may have contributed little to the spread of the fire. By the time the fire reached the roof, it had already spread so far within the wall cavity that much of the roof was exposed to fire around the same time and fire stopping beneath the roof tiles would have had little effect.

Unlike Grenfell, there will be no national public inquiry into the events surrounding the Richmond House fire. It was largely a local issue. There was no loss of life amongst the 60 residents, which included 17 children, or serious injuries. It was not a tower block. The building had already been fully evacuated.

More than two years on from the Grenfell fire, there was already a heightened alertness generally amongst residential building-owners and leaseholders of the risk of fire and its consequences. We can also be sure that Richmond House will not be the last fire caused either by defective materials or defective installation within a multi-occupied residential building. So it is about managing the risk.

What is certain to rumble on from the Richmond House fire is the legal fallout. Whilst we cannot be privy to the negotiations between lawyers representing residents and the original developer, it must be assumed that the former Richmond House residents will avoid some of the crippling financial liabilities faced by other residential leaseholders dealing with defective materials or construction, even where no actual fire has taken place. The fact that Richmond House was constructed as recently as 2011 must mean that the building was still under warranty at the time the 2019 fire occurred. And it must be assumed that the fire-damage itself would have been covered by buildings insurance. But there are some emotional losses which cannot be fully compensated. The following edited comments were found on Trustpilot:

> Two years ago I lost all my possessions to fire. Every keepsake from my past. Every photo of relatives who had passed away, including my parents. Everything I and my young children have ever owned. Everything that could ever remind me of my past.

6 The problem

> I was asleep in bed in my flat when the fire started. 20 minutes later it was gone and I was outside in my dressing gown with my four- and six-year-old in their pyjamas.

Who should read this book

This is intended to be a practical book to enable anyone concerned with the issue of fire safety in a multi-occupied residential building, of whatever height, to know exactly where they stand both legally – and financially. Its intended readership includes building-owners, managers, individual leaseholders, mortgage-lenders, buy-to-let landlords and anyone involved in the purchase or sale of a flat situated within a multi-occupied block. In this book we address the issue of fire-risk in relation to a multi-occupied residential building and how those remedial responsibilities (together with the associated costs) are apportioned between everyone affected. In this book we assess these issues in the following ways:

1 In Chapter 2, we assess the extent of the problem by reviewing and following up information and recommendations from the on-going Grenfell Inquiry (see below) and elsewhere as it emerges, beginning with the Part I Inquiry Report, published on 30 October 2019.
2 In Chapter 3, we provide a practical and detailed overview of the Fire Safety Order 2005, as amended by the Fire Safety Act 2021, and more recently by the Building Safety Act 2022, as being the principal overarching piece of legislation for building owners and managers.
3 We then review official guidance relating to fire safety within multi-occupied residential buildings.
4 In Chapter 7, we reference other legislation relevant to fire safety in a multi-occupied residential building, including the amended Building Regulation B4; as well as other regulations governing health and electricity safety, as well as fitness for habitation. We also make reference to the government's Building Safety Act 2022 which will impose additional duties on building-managers, mainly in relation to the provision of information.
5 We analyse the structure of a typical long-residential lease to assess how the legal responsibilities for fire safety and the costs of putting right existing building defects are split between a ground-landlord or management company and individual leaseholders. We also look at associated legislation intended to protect resident leaseholders from excessive service charges and how this might affect the costs of replacing defective cladding. This part of the book also looks at the common situation in which leaseholders are collectively their own landlord through their membership of a freehold management company, including situations where leaseholders have exercised their collective 'right to manage'.
6 We assess the extent to which it might be possible for building owners and leaseholders to transfer responsibility for the costs of rectifying

defective cladding onto a third party, such as the organisation responsible for installing the cladding or the National Housing Building Council or other warranty provider or the party originally at fault. This third party might also include central government, through a grant or a loan scheme.

7 In Chapter 11, we look at the extra layer of due diligence required on anyone proposing to buy or sell a flat in a block which might have defective cladding, as well as on anyone paid to represent a prospective buyer, or a prospective mortgage-lender, going forwards. When is a completed form ESW1 required? How much comfort does that completed form EWS1 provide? How easy is it to obtain one?

8 In Chapter 12, we look at the position of the property investor. This might be the small buy-to-let landlord buying a single flat to let as an investment. Or it could refer to the person who buys an entire block: perhaps one in which the need for expensive fire-safety works has already been identified.

9 We look in more detail at the help which the government might provide through its Building Safety Fund. We consider what that help is likely to cover and the terms on which such help is likely to be granted. At the time of writing, this is very much a work-in-progress in which there have been many encouraging government announcements but little in the way of detail.

10 Who is going to pay for it all? The government has no money of its own. That money has to be raised through taxation. We look at government proposals for a Residential Property Developer Tax to provide the funding required to remove existing defective cladding.

The Government's Building Safety Act 2022 is very much an 'enabling' Act, which means that the detail of the new legislation will be set out in later regulations. Though this legislation has reached the statute book, there may still be a further delay until its provisions take effect. However, this non-controversial Act will help to swing the balance of power towards leaseholders when it comes to providing clarity as to what ground-landlords and building-managers are required to do to make buildings safer and to deal fairly with leaseholders when it comes to re-charging the costs of remediation works.

In summary, the Building Safety Act 2022 provides for the appointment of a Building Safety Regulator and for the registration of 'higher-risk buildings' which are at least 18 metres in height or at least seven storeys and contain at least two residential units, for which there will be a duty for 'accountable persons' to appoint an 'accountable person'. It also makes amendments to the Fire Safety Order.

2 The Grenfell Inquiry

Like an inquest, a public inquiry has to be backward-facing. It picks over the remnants of a disaster to try to find out what went wrong. Who was to blame? Why were they to blame? What should they have done differently? Almost as an afterthought, that inquiry may also include recommendations for the future. To prevent a similar disaster happening again. That is also the position with the Grenfell Inquiry, which is chaired by the Right Hon. Sir Martin Moore-Bick and which published its Phase 1 Report on 30 October 2019, before being interrupted by the Covid pandemic.

We focus only on those sections of that Phase 1 Report which are of relevance to building-owners, leaseholders and their professional representatives going forward. *We regard Moore-Bick's Part 1 findings as particularly important as they provide a checklist of factors which can contribute to the spread of fire and hamper search-and-rescue operations in a high-rise building and which therefore need to be addressed in any regulatory risk-assessment. Note in particular the importance which Moore-Bick placed on fire-doors and the need for building-managers to ensure that self-closing devices are properly functioning at all times.* This Phase 1 Report is subdivided into the following six Parts, each of which is further sub-divided into chapters:

- Part 1 contains a broad introduction to the events of 14 June 2017 and describes Grenfell Tower, originally completed in 1974 and the subject of a refurbishment in 2015, and sets the scene. It also explains the principles then underpinning fire safety in high-rise residential buildings, which led to the adoption of a 'stay-put' strategy in response to fires occurring within individual flats. It also provides an overview of the 2015 Grenfell refurbishment, containing a description of the new cladding system, associated changes to the windows and their surrounds, as well as other building features that were intended to promote safety in the event of fire.
- Part 2 contains a detailed narrative account of the 2017 fire and the steps taken in response to it. That narrative, so far as it relates to the spread of fire, can be summarised as follows:

    a   00:54 fire reported in Flat 16, fourth floor;
    b   00:58 the first firefighters reach the Tower;

DOI: 10.1201/9781003291893-2

c   01:09 fire breaks out of Flat 16 into the exterior cladding and rapidly starts to climb the east façade;
d   01:17 fire reaches the roof and starts to spread horizontally;
e   02:00 flames travel across the north and east elevation of the Tower and start to spread around the crown and diagonally across the face of the building, affecting flats in the south-east and north-west corners;
f   02:20 flames start to spread to the south elevation;
g   02:50 fire spread horizontally across the south elevations out of the crown;
h   03:30 flames continue to spread across the south and west elevations of the Tower;
i   04:02 fires on the south and west elevations start to converge at the top of the southern corner of the west face;
j   08:07 the last survivor is evacuated from the building.

- Part 3 contains Moore-Bick's conclusions about the origin and development of the fire and how he viewed the response of the emergency services.
- Parts 4 and 5 contain recommendations arising out of earlier inquiry findings.
- Part 6 looks ahead to identify matters of particular importance on which the inquiry will concentrate its attention in Phase 2, for which, at the time of writing, a publication date has yet to be announced.

The fire most likely started as a result of an electrical fault in a large fridge-freezer in the kitchen of Flat 16. It is considered most likely to have entered the cladding as a result of hot smoke impinging on the uPVC window jamb, causing it to deform and collapse and thereby provide an opening into the cavity between the installation and the ACM cladding panels through which the flames and hot gases could pass.

An alternative, less-likely explanation, was that flames from the fire in the fridge-freezer passed through an open kitchen window and impinged on the ACM cladding panels above.

Once the fire had escaped from Flat 16, it spread rapidly up the east face of the Tower and then spread around the top of the building in both directions and down the sides until the advancing flame-fronts converged on the west face near the south-west corner, enveloping the entire building in under three hours. The principal reason why the flames spread so rapidly up, down and around the building was the presence of an aluminium composite material (ACM) rainscreen panels with polyethylene cores, which acted as a source of fuel.

The principal mechanism for the spread of the fire horizontally and downwards was the melting and dripping of burning polyethylene from the crown and from the spandrel and column panels, which ignited fires lower down the building. Those fires then travelled back up the building, thereby allowing the flame-front to progress diagonally across the face of the Tower. The presence of polyisocyanurate (PIR) and phenolic foam insulation boards behind the ACM panels, and perhaps components of the window surrounds, were found to contribute to the pace and extent of vertical flames spread. The crown was primarily responsible for the spread of the fire horizontally and the columns were a principal route of downwards fire-spread.

The fire on the outside of the building quickly entered many flats and smoke spread quickly through the interior of the building, which meant that effective compartmentalisation was lost at an early stage. Compartmentation failed because the intensity of the heat was such that the glass in the windows inevitably failed, allowing the fire to penetrate flats. Kitchen extractor fans also have a propensity to deform and become dislodged, providing a point of entry. Other key fire-protection measures inside the Tower failed.

Although some fire-doors held back the smoke, others did not. Some were left open and failed to close because they lacked effective self-closing devices. Other doors were broken down by firefighters or wedged open with firefighting equipment. Many lobbies had started to fill with smoke by 01.50 and some or all were significantly smoke-logged by 01.40. By 2.00 a.m. a significant number were heavily smoke-logged. Until 01:50 there was less smoke in the stairs, which had enabled 168 people to escape. After that time the stairs started to fill with smoke, particularly at lower levels. At some levels the smoke was thick and the heat considerable. By 2:00, the smoke in the stairs posed a risk to life but they were not absolutely impassable.

The inspector found compelling evidence that the external walls of the building failed to comply with requirement B4(1) of schedule 1 of the Building Regulations 2010 in that they did not adequately resist the spread of fire having regard to the height and position of the building. On the contrary, they actively promoted it.

In summary, the inspector found that the use of combustible materials in the external wall of Grenfell Tower, principally in the form of ACM rainscreen cladding, but also in the form of combustible installation, was the reason why the fire spread so quickly to the whole of the building. Subsequent surveys have established that similar materials to those used at Grenfell Tower have been used on over 400 other high-rise residential buildings in the country. The origin of the fire was itself no more than a typical kitchen fire. But what caused that fire to spread and to engulf the whole building was the proximity of combustible materials to the kitchen windows.

The inspector noted that no plans of the internal layout of the building had been made available to the London Fire Brigade until the later stages of the fire, though this did not hamper efforts to control the fire because each floor of the building above Level 3 was laid out in the same way. However, in a different block of flats, the lack of floor plans might easily have had far more serious consequences. *The inspector therefore recommended first of all that the owner and manager of every high-rise residential building be required by law to provide local fire and rescue services with up-to-date plans in both paper and electronic form of every floor of the building, identifying the location of key fire-safety systems. Second, that the managers of a high-rise building should be required by law to ensure that the building contains the premises information box, the contents of which must include up-to-date floor plans and information about the nature of any lift intended for use by the fire and rescue services.*

Firefighters attending the Grenfell Tower fire were unable to operate any mechanism that should have allowed them to take control of the lifts, which meant that they were unable to make use of the lifts in carrying out firefighting and search-and-rescue operations. It also meant that the occupants of the Tower were able to make use of the lifts in trying to escape, in some cases with fatal consequences. He therefore recommended that the owner and manager of every high-rise residential building be required by law to carry out regular inspections of any lifts that are designed to be used by firefighters in an emergency and to report the results of such inspections at monthly intervals to their local fire and rescue service. He also recommended that the owner and manager of every high-rise residential building be required by law to carry out regular tests of any mechanism which allows firefighters to take control of lifts and inform the local fire and rescue service at monthly intervals that they have done so.

As regards the evacuation of a high-rise building in case of fire, the inspector made the following recommendations (summarised):

- The government should develop national guidelines for the partial or total evacuation of high-rise residential buildings, to include the means of protecting fire-exit routes and procedures for evacuating persons unable to use the stairs in an emergency or who may require assistance.
- Fire and rescue services should develop policies for partial and total evacuation of high-rise residential buildings and training to support them.
- The owner and manager of every high-rise residential building should be required by law to draw up and keep under regular review evacuation plans, copies of which are to be provided in electronic and paper form and supplied to their local fire and rescue service and placed in an information box on the premises.
- All high-rise residential buildings now in existence or to be built in the future should be equipped with facilities for use by the fire and rescue services, enabling them to send an evacuation signal to the whole or a selected part of the building by means of sounders or similar devices.
- The owner and manager of every high-rise residential building should be required by law to prepare personal emergency evacuation plans (PEEPs) for all residents whose ability to self-evacuate may be compromised, such as persons with reduced mobility or cognition.
- The owner and manager of every high-rise residential building should be required by law to include up-to-date information about persons with

reduced mobility and their associated PEEPs in the premises information box.
- All fire and rescue services should be equipped with smoke hoods to assist in the evacuation of occupants through smoke-filled exit routes.

There was also much to be said in favour of householders obtaining fire blankets and fire extinguishers for their own use and, if they live in high-rise buildings, there is a strong argument that such equipment, if appropriately used, may protect not only the occupants of the flat in which the fire occurred but also the occupants of the building as a whole. However, another view expressed at the inquiry was that people should not be encouraged to fight fires themselves but should leave the building as quickly as possible and call the fire and rescue service. None of the inquiry experts supported the provision of fire extinguishers, hose reels or fire buckets, which had obvious potential for misuse.

Whilst the inspector accepted that sprinkler systems do have a valuable part to play in the overall scheme of fire safety, he did not consider that a sprinkler system would have suppressed the fire in Flat 16 or prevented it from escaping into the cladding.

The absence of floor numbers on the landings in the staircase at Grenfell Tower and the fact that floor numbers which had been marked did not reflect the additional floors created during the refurbishment, meant that firefighters were unable to identify floors clearly when carrying out firefighting or search-and-rescue operations within the building. *He therefore recommended that, going forward, in all high-rise buildings, floor numbers be clearly marked on each landing, within the stairways and in a prominent place in all lobbies in such a way as to be visible both in normal conditions and in low lighting or smoky conditions.*

The ability of residents to read and understand fire-safety instructions placed in the lobbies throughout a high-rise building is important because it helps to save lives. In the case of Grenfell Tower, fire-safety advice was prominently displayed in the lobbies but it was written only in English. The inspector therefore recommended that the owner and manager of every residential building containing separate dwellings, whether or not in a high-rise building, be required by law to provide fire-safety instructions, including instructions for evacuation, in a form that the occupants of the building can reasonably be expected to understand, taking into account the nature of the building and their knowledge of the occupants.

It had become apparent from the evidence obtained in Phase 1 of the inquiry that ineffective fire-precautions had allowed smoke and toxic gases to spread through the building more quickly than would have been expected. One important reason why the fire-doors failed to perform their essential function was the absence of effective self-closing devices, some of which were broken or had been disabled or removed. He considered that fire-doors play an essential role in preventing or inhibiting the spread of smoke and toxic gases and in preserving effective compartmentation of buildings.

Therefore, going forward, he recommended, first of all, that the owner and manager of every residential building containing separate dwellings, whether or not they are high-rise buildings, should carry out an urgent inspection of all the fire-doors to ensure that they comply with the applicable legislative standards. Second, he recommended that the owner and manager of every residential building containing separate dwellings be required by law to carry out checks not less than at three-monthly intervals to ensure that all fire-doors are fitted with effective self-closing devices and are in working order.

He also regarded effective fire-doors as particularly important in those high-rise buildings that are exposed to an increased risk of fire because the external walls currently incorporate unsafe cladding. The inspector accordingly recommended that all those who have responsibility, in whatever capacity, for the condition of the entrance doors to individual flats in high-rise residential buildings, whose external walls incorporate unsafe cladding, be legally required to ensure that such doors comply with current standards.

Whilst reference in the Part 1 Report to a high-rise building relates to a building which, in England and Wales, has been defined, for regulatory purposes, as buildings over 18 metres in height, the inspector noted that in Scotland the regulations had recently been changed so that the requirements relating to high-rise buildings applied to buildings over 11 metres in height. It is also an issue which he intends to address in the second part of the Grenfell Inquiry.

3 The Fire Safety Order (FSO)

When it comes to legal responsibility for fire safety within a building, the starting point has to be the *Fire Safety Order 2005 (FSO)*, which defines the legal responsibilities for the owner or manager of any building, other than a private dwelling house occupied by a single household. The remit of the 2005 Order has also been extended by the Fire Safety Act 2021, in response to fire-safety issues identified as a result of the Grenfell Tower fire, and which was brought into effect on 16 May 2022. There are also some prospective amendments included in the Building Safety Act 2022, which are addressed later in this chapter.

As originally drafted, the FSO was primarily concerned with non-residential premises. However, its remit has always extended to the communal parts of multi-occupied residential buildings, such as blocks of flats. The Fire Safety Act 2021 further extended the FSO's remit to the structural and external parts of multi-occupied residential buildings, to include external wall-cladding. But the duties which the FSO creates do not exist in isolation. The FSO has to be read together with the statutory guidance which accompanies it. It is also part of a wider legislative framework governing legal responsibilities for fire safety.

What is set out in this chapter is an explanation of how the FSO applies to the owners and managers of multi-occupied residential buildings. The two phrases which occur repeatedly throughout the FSO are 'responsible person' and 'relevant persons'. The 'responsible person' is the person or organisation deemed responsible for complying with the FSO responsibilities, which might be: a ground-landlord; a building-manager; an employer; or someone with a specific contractual responsibility. 'Relevant persons' are the people to whom the regulatory fire-safety duties are owed: which can be summarised as anyone resident or working in the premises or otherwise lawfully present, including anyone else in the immediate vicinity of the premises.

Another word used repeatedly throughout the FSO is 'competent', to describe someone who has sufficient training and experience or knowledge and other qualities to enable that person to undertake the fire-safety responsibilities which are assigned to them. Whilst a formal fire-safety qualification might evidence that the person has the required competence, the definition itself does not insist on possession of a recognised qualification. To be

DOI: 10.1201/9781003291893-3

'competent', a person must have both the ability and adequate structured training to carry out their fire-safety responsibilities.

The duties imposed by the FSO on a responsible persons fall into two types:

1   the employer's duty owed by a responsible person either to their own employees or to someone who is an employee of a third party or who is self-employed and working at the premises;
2   the duty owed by the responsible person to anyone else (other than employees) who is lawfully present in a building or in the immediate vicinity of that building. This would include the duties owed by a ground-landlord or building-manager to people living in the building.

Someone who is professionally managing a block of flats may owe duties of both types. They may owe a duty to their own employees, such as a caretaker or maintenance staff. But they will also owe duties to anyone resident in the building, as well as their visitors or anyone else with lawful business at the premises.

The FSO also has to be read together with the, frequently updated, Government Guidance, as collected together on the Home Office website: 'Fire-Safety Law and Guidance Documents for Business', as summarised in Chapter 4 of this book. In this chapter we have referred to the October 2007 Guidance Note No 1 to assist interpretation of the FSO. We refer to this as 'the No 1 Guidance'.

Summary of FSO duties

In summary, the FSO provides the following key duties on anyone responsible for the safety of any person lawfully present in a commercial or other multi-occupied building, including a residential block of flats:

1   To carry out a regulatory *risk assessment* in relation to the premises to which the FSO applies and to use the results of that risk assessment to guide compliance with the remaining provisions of the FSO.
2   Based on the risk assessment, to put in place *general fire-precautions*, including means of escape; provision and maintenance of firefighting equipment; and provision of information to persons affected.
3   *To identify risk due to the presence of any dangerous substances and, so far as it is possible to do so, to remove the dangerous substances or the risk associated with them.* Where the risks from dangerous substances cannot be removed entirely, the responsibility is then to manage that risk. Such dangerous substances could include flammable wall insulation on a block of flats.
4   Where there is more than one person with FSO responsibilities in respect of premises, there is a duty on those persons to cooperate with each other.

5   Although FSO duties are owed to everyone resident in or having lawful business at the premises, there are higher duties owed to employees.
6   *As well as the FSO itself, there is also a duty to pay due regard to official published guidance.*
7   To ensure that there are a sufficient number of 'competent' persons who have been adequately trained to oversee the carrying out of the FSO responsibilities and to deal with any emergency.
8   To keep the local fire and rescue authority informed as regards fire-safety arrangements, to the extent that the FSO requires.

FSO Articles and their definitions

Let us now look briefly at the Articles 3–50 of the FSO in detail.

Article 3: The responsible person: Who is responsible for compliance with the FSO?

The FSO generally places responsibility for compliance on a person having control of the premises to which the regulations apply. That responsible person could be an employer or the proprietor of a business, including a not-for-profit organisation. Or it could be the owner of the premises not connected to any particular business activity. Responsibility for compliance with the FSO may also be the responsibility of multiple parties or a shared responsibility.

The 'responsible person' as regards compliance with the FSO depends on whether the particular premises can be described as a 'workplace' or whether they are premises to which the FSO applies in some other capacity. As one would expect, it is the employer who is responsible for safety in the workplace to the extent that the workplace itself is under that employer's control.

Where the premises are not connected to any particular business activity, the responsible person is the owner of the premises. That 'owner' might be the freeholder of the building or it could be a particular leaseholder. It all depends on how the particular title to the land is structured.

Like other environmental legislation, 'ownership' is given a technical meaning. The FSO defines an 'Owner' as:

> The person for the time being receiving the rack rent of the premises in connection with which the word is used, whether on his own account or as agent or trustee for another person, or who would receive the rack rent if the premises were let at a rack rent.

So, for example, who would be the 'owner' of a block of 25 flats in which each of the flats had been sold off on separate 150-year leases, each at a fixed £50 annual ground-rent plus service charges? It would depend on which part of that multi-occupied building is our concern.

If we are talking about the interior of an individual flat, that responsibility would rest with the individual leaseholder, as being the person entitled to rent it out. But that 'ownership' would not normally extend to any part of the structure or exterior of the building.

Under modern leasehold law, ownership of that structure and exterior, as well as any communal parts of the building, such as entrance lobbies, corridors, lifts and stairways, would, in most cases, remain with the ground-landlord, even though in reality there is no way in which those functional parts of a multi-occupied building could be separately rented out. And certainly not at a market rent.

It may not only be the ground-landlord named on the deeds who is the 'owner'. That 'owner' definition also extends to a managing-agent of the owner. It could also extend to a contractor who has control of any part of the premises in connection with the carrying out of their trade or business. Some parts of the building might also be considered a 'workplace', such as a boiler-room, store cupboard, or perhaps even a caretaker's flat.

Finally, it is important to note Article 5(3), which extends responsibility for compliance beyond the defined 'responsible person' (see above), to include any other person who has, to any extent, control of the premises so far as the requirements relate to matters under their control.

Article 5(4) extends the compliance responsibilities further to anyone having a tenancy or other contractual responsibility, as regards either the maintenance or repair of the premises, or as regards its safety.

Where there is more than one person with duties under the FSO, Paragraph 40 of the No 1 Guidance creates an expectation that the enforcing authority will use discretion in deciding what enforcement action to take and against whom.

Article 5 (and Article 31(10)): To what premises does the FSO apply?

As extended by the Fire Safety Act 2021, and as defined in the FSO, the legal responsibilities imposed by the order on the owners and managers of premises now apply to any of the following premises:

- any non-domestic premises (which are defined to include any workplace; any vehicle, vessel, aircraft or hovercraft; any installation on land; and any temporary or moveable structure);
- the structure, external walls (including doors and windows in those walls and anything attached to the exterior of those walls, including balconies) of any building containing two or more sets of domestic premises (added by the Fire Safety Act 2021);
- all doors between domestic premises and common parts in a building containing two or more sets of domestic premises (added by the Fire Safety Act 2021);
- a house which is not occupied as a single private dwelling (for example, a house in multiple occupation);

- the communal parts of a multi-occupied residential building, such as entrance lobbies; lifts; corridors; common rooms; stairways; or any other part of a building which residents are entitled to share;
- any part of a residential building which could be described as a workplace, such as a boiler room or maintenance cupboard. Maybe even a caretaker's flat.
- an individual flat situated within a multi-occupied residential building.

The position of individual flat owners under the FSO is ambiguous. On the one hand, the FSO places primary responsibility for carrying out regulatory risk assessments and the implementation of fire-precautions on the manager of the building. On the other hand, individual flat owners are required to cooperate with the implementation of fire-precautions put in place either by the building-manager or fire and rescue authority. This might include a requirement to vacate individual flats in response to a Prohibition Notice issued by the local fire and rescue authority if there is a significant fire-risk (see below).

Article 6 (and Article 31(10)): To what premises does the FSO not apply?

Article 6 makes clear that *the FSO does not apply* to a house occupied by a single household. The word 'house' has to be given its natural meaning, whether it is detached, semi-detached, or terraced. A principal legal difference between a house and a residential apartment, is that in most cases a house is owned freehold, whereas a flat is occupied on lease. With a freehold house, no-one else is involved. There are other specific statutory exemptions for ships, open farmland and rolling-stock.

What are the duties under the FSO?

The primary fire-safety duties under the FSO for employers, owners, agents, tenants, building-managers and contractors are set out in Part 2 of the FSO (Articles 8–22 as well as any supplemental regulations made pursuant to Article 24).

Article 8: General fire precautions

Article 8 requires employers to take such general fire precautions as will ensure, so far as reasonably practicable, the safety of their employees, and for non-employers, a slightly lower responsibility to take such general fire precautions that may reasonably be required in the circumstances to ensure that the premises are safe.

The term 'general fire precautions' is defined in Article 4 to mean: measures to reduce the risk of fire on the premises and the spread of fire; means of escape; means for fighting fires; measures for detecting fire and giving warnings;

adequate arrangements relating to the instruction and training of employees and other measures to mitigate the effects of a fire.

Paragraph 43 of the No 1 Guidance states that the definition is intended to create clear demarcation between general fire precautions and other special precautions related to work processes.

Paragraph 53 of the No 1 Guidance explains that Article 8 imposes on the responsible person the duty to implement the preventative and protective measures evaluated in the risk assessment carried out pursuant to Article 9 (see below).

Article 9: Mandatory risk assessments

Article 9 imposes on the 'responsible person' a requirement to carry out a mandatory risk assessment: namely, a suitable and sufficient assessment of the risks to which 'relevant persons' are exposed, to identify the general fire precautions the responsible person needs to undertake to comply with the requirements and prohibitions imposed by the FSO.

Where there is likely to be a dangerous substance present on the premises (note: this might include flammable wall-cladding), that fire-risk assessment must include consideration of the matters set out in Part 1 of Schedule 1 of the FSO, which can be summarised as follows:

a   The hazardous properties of the substance.
b   Supplier safety information.
c   If employment is involved, the circumstances of the work, including: special, technical and organisational measures and the substances used and their possible interactions; the amount of the substance involved; where the work will involve more than one dangerous substance, the risk presented by such substances in combination; and the arrangements for the safe handling, storage and transport of dangerous substances and of waste containing dangerous substances.
d   Activities, such as maintenance, with a potential for a higher level of risk.
e   The effect of FSO measures which have been or will be taken.
f   The likelihood that an explosive atmosphere will occur and its persistence.
g   The likelihood that ignition sources, including electrostatic discharges, will be present and become active and effective.
h   The scale of the anticipated effects.
   i   Any places which are, or can be connected via openings to, places in which explosive atmospheres may occur.
i   Such additional safety information as the responsible person may need to complete if they employ a young person.

Article 9 risk assessments must be regularly reviewed by the responsible person and kept up to date. Changes must be made where there is reason to suspect that it is no longer valid or that there has been a significant change in the matters to which it relates, including when the premises, special, technical or organisational measures, or organisation of the work undergo significant changes, extensions or conversions. Note that the FSO is not prescriptive as to the time an existing risk assessment remains valid. Instead there is a rolling responsibility on the person responsible to be alert to the need to keep it under review and make changes where required.

Surprisingly, a regulatory obligation to formally record the findings of a fire-risk assessment is only required under Article 9(6) in any of the following circumstances: there are five or more employees; there is in force any regulatory licence in relation to the premises; or there is in force an 'Alterations Notice' (see Article 29) in relation to the premises.

Where a formal record of the fire-risk assessment is required, the information to be recorded must include: the significant findings of the assessment, including measures which have been or will be taken pursuant to the FSO; and details of any group of persons identified as being particularly at risk.

Article 9(8) prevents any new work activity involving a dangerous substance from starting unless a risk assessment has been made and measures required by the FSO have been implemented.

Paragraph 56 of the No 1 Guidance explains that the nature of the risk assessment will vary according to the type and use of the premises, the persons using the premises, and the risks associated with that use. Also that a risk assessment should be reviewed regularly to keep it up to date, valid and reflect any significant changes that may have taken place. Advice given in paragraph 62 of the No 1 Guidance is that the suitability of a risk assessment and its recording, are reliant on its ease of understanding. Particularly in complex buildings, the risk assessment may need to incorporate plans, showing general fire precaution arrangements, where it is not possible to identify matters clearly in the narrative of the assessment.

When it is brought into force, Section 156 of the Building Safety Act 2022 will introduce a new Article 9A, which will prevent the Responsible Person from appointing anyone to assist them in making an Article 9 Assessment who is not 'competent' as defined and to ensure that, where more than one assistant is appointed, that those assistants cooperate with each other.

Articles 10 and 11: Minimising fire safety risk in premises to which the FSO applies

Article 10 states that where the responsible person implements any preventive and protective measures, they must do so on the basis of the principles specified in Part 3 of Schedule 1, namely:

a   avoiding risks;
b   evaluating risks which cannot be avoided;
c   combating risks at source;

d   adapting to technical progress;
e   replacing the dangerous by the non-dangerous or less dangerous;
f   developing a coherent overall prevention policy which covers technology, organisation of work and the influence of factors relating to the working environment;
g   giving collective protective measures priority over individual protective measures;
h   giving appropriate instructions to employees.

Note: Principle (e) 'Replacing the dangerous by the non-dangerous or less dangerous' would appear particularly relevant when it comes to flammable wall-cladding in any building.

Paragraphs 63–66 of the No 1 Guidance explain that these eight principles express the ethos of the FSO as a prevention and mitigation regime where actually preventing fire and mitigating its effects when it happens are as important as a means of escape and traditional fire precautions. When it comes to mitigation, enforcing authorities will consider whether the responsible person has done everything reasonably practicable to reduce the risk of fire and of a fire developing if it breaks out. In following some of these measures, responsible persons need to consider health and safety regulations and measures regarding work processes and dangerous substances.

Article 11 requires the responsible person to make and give effect to appropriate arrangements for the effective planning, organisation control, monitoring and review of preventative and protective measures. Paragraph 68 of the No 1 Guidance states that the purpose of Article 11 is to require effective management and control of the fire-safety arrangements in the affected premises. Paragraphs 67–69 of the No 1 Guidance explain that the Article 11 duty gives rise in the first instance to the requirement for an emergency plan, including measures to ensure the effective operation of the plan and for ongoing checks of the appropriateness of the plan and other measures. These arrangements will typically also relate to measures required by other Articles of the FSO.

Article 12: Responsibilities as regards dangerous substances

Where a dangerous substance is present in or on the premises, Article 12 requires the responsible person to ensure that risk related to the presence of the substances is either eliminated or reduced so far as is reasonably practicable.

In complying with this duty, the responsible person must, so far as reasonably practicable, replace a dangerous substance, or the use of a dangerous substance, with a substance or process which either eliminates or reduces the risk to relevant persons.

Where it is not reasonably practicable to eliminate such risks, the responsible person must so far as reasonably practicable, apply measures consistent with the risk assessment and appropriate to the nature of the activity or operation, including measures specified in Part 4 of Schedule 1 of the FSO to control the risk of fire and mitigate the detrimental effects of a fire. The responsible person must also arrange for the safe handling, storage and transport of dangerous substances and of waste containing dangerous substances, and ensure that conditions for ensuring the elimination and reduction of risk are maintained.

Part 4 of Schedule 1 lists the specific measures to be taken by the responsible person in respect of dangerous substances namely:

1. In order of priority to: reduce the quantity of dangerous substances to a minimum; avoid or minimise the release of a dangerous substance; control the release of a dangerous substance at source; prevent the formation of an explosive atmosphere, including the application of appropriate ventilation; ensure that any release of a dangerous substance giving rise to a risk is suitably collected, safely contained, removed to a safe place or otherwise rendered safe. The responsible person must also take measures to avoid: ignition sources including electrostatic discharges; such other adverse conditions as would result in harmful physical effects from a dangerous substance; and segregate incompatible dangerous substances.

2. The responsible person must ensure that mitigation measures: reduce to a minimum the number of persons exposed; avoid the propagation of fires or explosions; provide explosion or pressure relief arrangements; provide explosion suppression equipment; provide plant which is constructed to withstand the pressure likely to be produced by an explosion; and provide suitable personal protective equipment.

3. It requires the responsible person to ensure that: premises are designed, constructed and maintained so as to reduce risk; suitable special, technical and organisational measures are designed, constructed, assembled, installed, provided and used so as to reduce risk; special, technical and organisational measures are maintained in an efficient state, in efficient working order and good repair. This paragraph also requires the responsible person to ensure that equipment and protective systems meet the following requirements: where power failure can give rise to the spread of additional risk, equipment and protective systems must be able to be maintained in a safe operational state independently of the rest of the plant in the event of power failure; there must be provided some means of manual override for shutting down equipment and protective systems incorporated within automatic processes which deviate from the intended operating conditions, provided that the provision or use of such manual override does not compromise safety. On operation of emergency shutdown, accumulated energy must be dissipated as quickly and as safely as possible or isolated so that it does no longer constitute a hazard and necessary measures must be taken to prevent confusion between connected devices. Where work is carried out in hazardous places or involves hazardous activities, the responsible person must ensure that appropriate

systems of work are applied including: the issuing of written instructions for the carrying out of work and a system of permits to work, with such permits being issued by a person with responsibility for this function before the work starts.

Under the heading 'Additional emergency measures in respect of dangerous substances', Article 16 (see below) requires a responsible person to put in place measures to ensure the safety of relevant persons where there is an accident, incident or emergency related to the presence of a dangerous substance. The exception is where the risk assessment shows that the quantity is so small that there is only a slight risk to relevant persons and that the measures the responsible person has taken to comply with their duty under Article 12 (elimination or reduction of risks from dangerous substances) are sufficient to control the at risk.

Note: Although it is clear that Article 12 was not originally written with dangerous cladding in mind, these obligations would seem particularly relevant for anyone responsible for the safe management of a block of flats. That 'someone' could be a ground-landlord; a managing-agent; or perhaps even the leaseholders themselves acting collectively through a management company. Note also that the requirement to remove unsafe cladding or other materials is not absolute but depends on what is 'reasonably practicable' in the circumstances. What is absolute is the obligation on a building-owner or manager to carry out the required risk assessment and do what it can to ensure the fire safety of residents as well as anyone else who is lawfully on the premises or within its immediate vicinity. Where the immediate removal of unsafe cladding on a building is, for any reason, not reasonably practicable, something else needs to be put in its place as an interim measure to ensure the safety of residents and others visiting the building. Those other measures might include a 'waking watch', where someone takes 24-hour responsibility for patrolling a building and alerting residents if a fire breaks out.

Article 13: Firefighting and fire detection

So far as is necessary to safeguard relevant persons, Article 13 requires the responsible person to ensure that premises are appropriately equipped with firefighting equipment, fire-detectors and alarms. Non-automatic firefighting equipment must be easily accessible, simple to use and indicated by signs.

What is appropriate in the circumstances is to be determined having regard to the dimensions and use of the premises, equipment used on the premises, the physical and chemical properties of substances likely to be present and the maximum number of people who may be present at any one time. The responsible person must also, where necessary, implement firefighting measures in the premises which are adapted to the nature of the activities carried on there and the size of the premises concerned. They must also nominate sufficient competent persons to implement those measures and ensure that their training and available equipment are adequate, taking into account the size of the premises and the specific hazards involved in the premises. The responsible person must also make sufficient contacts with the external emergency services, particularly as regards firefighting, rescue work, first-aid and emergency medical care.

Paragraph 73 of the No 1 Guidance states that firefighting equipment should be considered as a means of both prevention and protection and suggests that some form of firefighting equipment will be necessary in almost all cases.

Article 14: Emergency routes and exits

Where necessary to safeguard the safety of relevant persons, Article 14 requires the responsible person to ensure that routes to emergency exits, as well as the exits themselves, are kept clear at all times.

Emergency routes and exits must lead as directly as possible to a place of safety and, in the event of danger, make it possible for persons to evacuate as quickly and as safely as possible. The number, distribution and dimensions of emergency routes and exits must be adequate having regard to the use, equipment and dimensions of the premises and the maximum number of persons who may be present at any one time. *Emergency doors must open in the direction of escape. Sliding or revolving doors must not be used for emergency exits and must not be so locked or fastened that they cannot easily and immediately be opened by anyone who may need to use them in an emergency.*

Emergency routes and exits must be indicated by signs and those requiring illumination must be provided with emergency lighting of adequate intensity in case of failure of normal lighting.

Article 15: Procedures for serious and imminent danger and for danger areas

Article 15 requires the responsible person to maintain appropriate procedures, including fire-drills, to be followed in the event of serious and imminent danger and also to nominate a sufficient number of competent people to implement those procedures, so far as they relate to the evacuation of people from the premises and also to ensure that no-one has access to any area which is necessary to restrict access on grounds of safety, unless that person has received adequate safety instruction.

So far as is practicable, anyone exposed to serious and imminent danger must be informed of the nature of the hazard and of the steps taken to protect them from it. Procedures must also enable such persons to stop work and immediately go to a place of safety in the event of their being exposed to serious, imminent and unavoidable danger. Save in exceptional circumstances and for duly specified and substantiated reasons, such persons must also be prevented from resuming work in any situation where there is still a serious and imminent danger.

Article 16: Additional emergency measures in respect of dangerous substances

To safeguard the safety of relevant persons arising from an accident, incident or emergency relating to the presence of a dangerous substance, Article 16 requires the responsible person to ensure that:

- Information on emergency arrangements is available, including details of relevant work hazards and hazard identification arrangements as well as information about specific hazards likely to arise at the time of an accident, incident or emergency.
- There are suitable warning and other communication systems established to enable an appropriate response, including remedial actions and rescue operations, to be made immediately when an event occurs.
- Where necessary, before explosion conditions are reached, visual or audible warnings are given and relevant persons withdrawn.
- Where the risk assessment indicates it is necessary, escape facilities are provided and maintained to ensure that, in the event of danger, relevant persons can leave promptly and safely.

The above information must also be made available to accident and emergency services to enable such services to prepare their own response procedures and precautionary measures. Such information must also be displayed at the premises unless the results of the risk assessment make it unnecessary.

In the event of a fire arising from an accident, incident or emergency relating to a dangerous substance, the responsible person must ensure that immediate steps are taken to: mitigate the effects of the fire; restore the situation to normal; and inform relevant persons who may be affected. Only persons essential to carrying out of repairs and other necessary work are then permitted in the affected area and they must be provided with appropriate protective equipment and clothing. The only circumstances in which the Article 16 duties do not apply are where the results of the risk assessment show that because of the quantity of each dangerous substance, there is only a slight risk to relevant persons and that compliance with such measures as are required under Article 12 is sufficient to control the risk.

Article 17: Maintenance of firefighting equipment

So far as is necessary to safeguard relevant persons, Article 17 requires the responsible person to ensure that any facilities, equipment and devices provided, either under the FSO or any other legislative requirement, are maintained in an efficient state, in efficient working order and in good repair. Where the premises to which the FSO relates form part of a larger building, the responsible person may make arrangements with the occupier of other parts of the building to ensure the maintenance of firefighting equipment and associated facilities.

What this means is that a ground-landlord responsible for the common parts as well as the structure and exterior of a block of flats can enter into maintenance arrangements with individual flat-owners. In those circumstances, Article 17(4) would place the owner of that flat under a duty to cooperate with the ground-landlord or other building-manager in making those arrangements. Where that flat is occupied by someone other than the leaseholder (such as a tenant), the duty to cooperate extends to both the leaseholder as well as the person in actual occupation of the flat.

Paragraph 85 of the No 1 Guidance advises that although there are no direct criminal offences associated with a failure by the occupier of private domestic premises to cooperate with the landlord as regards maintenance of a common fire precaution, any contract or agreement between that private occupier and the building-manager or landlord should allow access to the responsible person to enable maintenance of any fire-safety provisions extending from the common parts to the domestic premises.

Article 18: Safety assistance

Article 18 requires the responsible person to appoint sufficient competent people to assist in carrying out the required preventative and protective measures and also ensure that those appointees can operate sufficiently with each other.

Paragraphs 89 and 90 of the No 1 Guidance explain that the level of necessary competence will vary according to the nature and complexity of the premises.

Basic training or use of recognized guidance together with a reasonable knowledge of the premises may well suffice for many micro, small and medium-sized premises. However, where premises are high-risk, large or complex, a higher level of competence is likely to be necessary. The need for specific competence in specialist areas, such as installation and maintenance of computerised fire detection and warning systems which are designed to suit the premises, should be considered. Although third-party accreditation schemes can indicate competence in a given specialist area, other means can be used. Care should be taken to ensure that where non-accredited companies are used, the level of competence is not compromised.

Article 19: Provision of information to employees

Article 19 of the FSO requires the responsible person to provide their employees with comprehensible and relevant information on: identified risks; preventative and protective measures; fire-drills and associated procedures, together with the identities of appointed fire-wardens; the duty of responsible persons to cooperate with each other and coordinate their fire-safety responsibilities.

Note that whilst the requirement to provide detailed information under this Article 19 does not extend beyond employees, the general Article 8 duty of care will necessitate appropriate information and instruction being drawn to the attention of other relevant persons.

Article 20: Provision of information to employers and the self-employed

The responsible person must ensure that the employer of anyone from an outside organisation working on the premises is provided with comprehensible and relevant information on the risks to those employees and the preventative and protective measures taken by the responsible person.

That information must also include sufficient detail to enable the other employer to identify any person nominated to implement evacuation procedures in relation to those employees. For anyone who is self-employed, the responsible person must ensure that they are also provided with appropriate instructions and comprehensible and relevant information regarding any risks. The responsible person must also take reasonable steps to ensure that both external employees and the self-employed receive sufficient information to enable them to identify anyone nominated to implement fire evacuation procedures. Paragraph 99 of the No 1 Guidance explains the need to consider practicality and gives the example of the postal worker who visits premises daily.

Article 21: Training

Article 21 requires a responsible person to ensure that their employees are provided with adequate safety training both at the time they are first employed and again on their being exposed to new or increased risks; on being transferred or being given a change of responsibilities; where they are introduced to new work equipment or there is any change respecting existing work equipment; the introduction of new technology; or the introduction of a new system of work or changes to an existing system of work.

That training must include suitable and sufficient instruction and training on appropriate precautions and actions to be taken by the employee to safeguard that employee and other relevant persons on the premises. Such training must be repeated as appropriate and adapted to take account of any new risks or change to risks to the safety of employees.

Paragraph 101 of the No 1 Guidance discusses the status of volunteers and whether this itself is sufficient to become a contract of employment, having regard to the fact that payment is not necessary for a contract to be valid. Some volunteers may therefore need to be considered as employees and receive appropriate training. In case of doubt, specific legal advice should be sought.

When it is brought into force, Section 156 of the Building Safety Act 2022 will introduce Article 21A imposing a new requirement for a building containing two or more sets of domestic premises, that the 'responsible person' must give residents comprehensible and relevant information about: risks identified by the risk assessment; preventative and protective measures; the name and address of the responsible person to which official notices and other documents can be sent; the identity of anyone appointed by the responsible person to assist them in making or reviewing an Article 9 assessment; the identity of anyone nominated by the responsible person under Article 13(3)(b); any other matters specified in regulations.

Article 22: Cooperation and coordination

Article 22 states that where two or more responsible persons share fire-safety responsibilities, they must cooperate with each other, take all reasonable steps to coordinate the carrying-out of their responsibilities and keep each other informed as regards risks to relevant persons. In premises where there is an explosive atmosphere, the responsible person with overall responsibility must coordinate the implementation of fire-safety measures to protect relevant persons from any risk from the explosive atmosphere.

When it is brought into force, Section 156 of the Building Safety Act 2022 will introduce an additional Article 22A (provision of information to new responsible person), which will apply when regulatory responsibilities are transferred from one person to another. A new Article 22B, headed 'Cooperation with Accountable Person', which applies to higher-risk buildings, will require the responsible person to take reasonable steps to ascertain whether there are other accountable persons in relation to the premises, in which case they must cooperate with each accountable person in carrying out their duties under the Building Safety Act 2022.

Article 23: General duties of employees at work

Article 23 places a direct responsibility on every employee to take reasonable care for their own safety as well as regards the safety of other relevant persons who may be affected by their acts or omissions. Employees must also cooperate with the employer as regards any fire-safety duties imposed on that employer and inform that employer or any other employee with specific fire-safety responsibilities, of any work situation which the employee reasonably considers represents a serious and immediate danger to safety and anything reasonably considered to represent a shortcoming in the employer's safety-protection arrangements.

Article 24: Power to make regulations about fire precautions

Article 24 of the FSO gives the Secretary of State power to make additional regulations as to the precautions which need to be taken or observed in relation to fire-risk. To implement certain Grenfell Inquiry recommendations, the Fire Safety (England) Regulations 2022 were laid before Parliament on 18 May 2022 and are scheduled to take effect on 23 January 2023. More information about these prospective legislative requirements is provided at the end of this chapter.

Articles 25–36: Enforcement of fire safety requirements

Primary responsibility for compliance with the FSO is placed on the Fire and Rescue Authority for the area within which the premises are situated (Article 25). Fire and rescue authorities are broadly defined as county councils and unitary authorities (meaning those administrative areas within England and Wales where local authority functions are not split between counties and districts but are instead combined into a single local authority). The Secretary of State may also establish combined fire and rescue authorities as stand-alone public bodies.

Lancashire Combined Fire Authority provides an example of such an independent body, comprising 25 elected members from three councils. The principal exception is Greater London where such responsibilities are now the function of the London Fire Commissioner.

Article 26 requires every enforcing authority to enforce the provisions of the FSO and any associated regulations and for that purpose may appoint inspectors. In carrying out its duties, the enforcement-authority must also have regard to any guidance issued by the Secretary of State.

Article 27 empowers a fire-inspector to do anything necessary to ensure compliance with the FSO. This includes specific power to do any of the following at a reasonable time:

- To enter premises and to carry out an inspection, to the extent that such entry and inspection can be affected without use of force.
- To make enquiries to ascertain, as regards any premises, whether the provisions of the FSO apply to those premises and, if so, whether its provisions are being complied with.
- To identify who is the responsible person in relation to premises.
- To require the production of records (including plans) maintained under the FSO for the purposes of examination or inspection and to take copies. Where information is recorded in a computerised format, the inspector may require the provision of extracts.
- To require any person having responsibilities in relation to any premises to provide such facilities and assistance as is necessary to enable the inspector to exercise their fire-safety functions.
- To take samples of any articles or substances found in any premises to ascertain their flammability or fire resistance.
- To test or cause to be dismantled or subject to any process or test, any article or substance found in premises which appears dangerous, but only so far as is necessary to damage or destroy such an article or substance.

Article 27(2) requires an inspector, if required when visiting premises, to produce evidence of the inspector's authority.

Before exercising any power to dismantle, adapt, test, damage or destroy any item which is perceived to be dangerous, Article 27(3) states that the inspector must, if requested by any responsible person who is present, require those steps to be taken in the presence of that responsible person. Where there is present an item or substance which appears dangerous, Article 27(4) requires an inspector to consult appropriate persons to enable the inspector to ascertain what dangers, if any, there may be in doing anything which the inspector proposes to do.

Article 29: Alterations Notices

The effect of an Alterations Notice is to require the responsible person to notify the fire and rescue authority of any proposed changes to high-risk premises before making those changes. The terms of the notice may also require the recipient to send details of their fire-safety risk assessments.

Article 29 allows an enforcing authority to serve an 'Alterations Notice' if it thinks that the premises are either a serious risk to relevant persons, whether due to the features of the premises, their use, any hazard present or other circumstances, or may constitute such a risk if the changes are made to the premises or the use to which they are put.

An Alterations Notice must state the enforcing authority's opinion that there is a serious risk and specify the matters which, in their opinion, constitutes that risk or may constitute such a risk if a change is made to the premises or use to which the premises are put.

Where an Alterations Notice has been served, the responsible person must, before making a change to the premises or to the services, fittings or equipment within or on the premises, notify the enforcing authority of those proposed changes. The requirement to notify also applies if there will be any increase in the quantities of dangerous substances present, or any proposed change in the use of the premises. An Alterations Notice may also include a requirement that the responsible person takes all reasonable steps to notify its terms to any other person who has FSO duties in relation to the premises and record the significant findings of any risk assessment, including measures which have been or will be taken by the responsible person, and identify any group of persons who are especially at risk.

Before making any proposed changes to the premises, the responsible person may then be required to provide to the enforcing authority a copy of that risk assessment and a summary of the proposed changes to be made to the existing general fire precautions. The issue of an Alterations Notice does not affect the ability of the enforcing authority to serve an Enforcement Notice or a Prohibition Notice in respect of premises (see below).

Paragraph 130 of the No 1 Guidance explains that the purpose of an Alterations Notice is twofold. First, it is to assist enforcing authorities in maintaining a risk-based inspection programme by highlighting potentially high-risk premises where risk levels may change and affect the outcomes of an earlier fire-risk assessment. Second, it notifies the responsible person that the enforcing authority considers the premises to be of high or potentially high risk.

Paragraph 136 states that an Alterations Notice might be appropriate for buildings which rely on critical fire protection elements, such as sprinklers, smoke ventilation and associated automatic fire detection; buildings where a fire-engineered solution has been incorporated within the building design to satisfy the functional requirements of the Building Regulations; or poorly managed buildings that are prone to regular fluctuations of risk or layout or occupancy.

Article 30: Enforcement Notices

Where there are significant failures to comply with the requirements of the FSO, the fire and rescue authority has the power to issue an Enforcement Notice on the responsible person.

Article 30 (2) states that an Enforcement Notice must:

- state its opinion that there has been a failure to comply with the FSO and explain why it is of that opinion;
- specify the provisions of the FSO which have not been complied with;
- require the recipient of the notice to take steps to remedy the failure within a stated compliance period, not less than 28 days after service of the notice.

Article 30(3) states that an Enforcement Notice may include directions as to the measures the enforcing authority considers necessary to remedy the failure and may also provide measures in the alternative, so as to give the recipient of the notice a choice between different ways of remedying the contravention. But note that this is subject to Article 36 of the FSO (see below) which enables the enforcing authority and the recipient of the notice to agree to refer any dispute as to the requirements to the Secretary of State for determination.

Article 30(7) enables the enforcing authority to withdraw an Enforcement Notice at any time before the expiration of the period for compliance. Where a statutory appeal against the notice is not already pending, the enforcing authority also has the power to extend or further extend the specified compliance period.

Article 31: Prohibition Notices

Article 31 enables the enforcing authority to serve a Prohibition Notice where it is of the opinion that the current use of the premises involves a risk to relevant persons which is so serious that it ought to be prohibited or restricted. Of specific relevance to that assessment of risk includes anything affecting escape from the premises in the event of fire.

A Prohibition Notice must: state the enforcing authority's opinion that the current use involves serious risk; specify the matters which it perceives gives rise to that risk and direct that the use to which the Prohibition Notice relates is prohibited or restricted to such extent as may be specified in the notice until the specified matters have been remedied. A Prohibition Notice may also include directions as to what measures have to be taken to remedy the specified matters and such measures may be framed in a way which gives the recipient of the notice a choice between different solutions.

Article 31(5) states that a Prohibition Notice can take effect immediately if the enforcing authority considers that the risk of serious personal injury is imminent. In any other case, the Prohibition Notice will take effect at the end of the specified period for compliance.

Before serving a Prohibition Notice in relation to a house in multiple occupation (as defined by the Housing Act 2004) and so far as it is practicable to do so, the enforcing authority must also notify the local housing authority of its intention to serve the Notice and the use which it intends to prohibit or restrict.

Article 31(10) is of particular importance as it enables an enforcing authority to issue a Prohibition Notice in relation to domestic premises, other than a house which is occupied by a single household.

Part 4: Offences and appeals

Article 32: Offences and penalties

Article 32 lists a range of criminal offences and penalties consequent on a person's failure to comply with their regulatory responsibilities under the FSO. *The most serious (Article 32 (1)) offence relates to a person's failure to carry out their FSO duties where that failure places someone at risk of death or serious injury in case of fire, and which is punishable by an unlimited fine or imprisonment for up to two years.* Punishable by similar penalties are a failure to comply with the requirements contained in an Alterations Notice; an Enforcement Notice; or a Prohibition Notice.

However, Article 32(2) also creates other offences of an administrative nature as well as a range of lesser offences which can apply to anyone, not just the 'responsible person' tasked with implementing the FSO duties. These additional Article 32(2) offences can be summarised as follows:

a   Failure to comply with Article 23 (general duties of employees) where that failure places relevant persons at risk of death or serious injury in case of fire.
b   Knowingly making a false entry in any register, a book, notice or other document required to be kept, served or given under the FSO.
c   Knowingly or recklessly giving false information in purported compliance with any obligation to give information under the FSO, including evidence of that person's authority.
d   Intentionally obstructing an inspector in the exercise of performance of their powers or duties under the FSO.

e   Failing, without reasonable excuse, to comply with any obligations to provide an inspector with documents or to provide other assistance which that person is obliged to provide to that inspector,
f   Intentionally pretending to be an inspector.
g   Failing to comply with a prohibition imposed by Article 40 (see below, duty not to charge employees).
h   Failing to comply with any prohibition or restriction imposed by a Prohibition Notice.

Anyone proven guilty of an offence under Article 32(2)(a) is liable to a fine of an unlimited amount. Anyone guilty of an offence under Article 32 (2)(b), (c); (d) or (g) is liable on summary conviction to a fine not exceeding Level 5 on the standard scale (which now means a fine of an unlimited amount). Anyone proven guilty of an offence under Article 2(2)(e) or (f) is liable on summary conviction to a fine not exceeding Level 3 on the standard scale (which means a maximum fine of £1,000).

Criminal liability also extends to any company director or other senior officer who is proved to have connived or otherwise been at fault in relation to that offence. Article 32(11) also makes clear that an employer cannot escape criminal liability by shifting blame for the offence onto an employee or other person nominated by the employer to undertake any FSO function.

Articles 33 and 34: The reasonable precautions defence

With two exceptions, Article 33 provides a statutory defence for anyone charged with an offence under Article 32 of the FSO who is able to prove that they took all reasonable precautions and exercised all due diligence to avoid commission of the offence. The two exceptions to which the statutory defence is not available are, first, the general Article 8(1)(a) duty to take such general fire precautions as will ensure, so far as is reasonably practicable, the safety of employees. Second, the general Article 12 duty on a responsible person to ensure that risk to relevant persons related to the presence of a dangerous substance is either eliminated or reduced, so far as is reasonably practicable.

The deliberate exclusion of Articles 8(1)(a) and 12 from the statutory Article 33 defence might be to avoid legislative duplication, as those particular offences are not themselves strict liability but incorporate a 'reasonableness test' within their respective definitions.

Article 34 makes clear that anyone seeking to rely on an Article 33 'reasonable precautions' defence must provide evidence to substantiate that defence. It is not enough simply to assert that reasonable precautions have been taken and then challenge the prosecution to disprove that assertion. In this respect, Article 34 follows the general law as set out in Section 101 of the Magistrates Courts Act 1980 which states that where a defendant relies on any exception, exemption, proviso, excuse or qualification, the burden of proving that exception, exemption, proviso or qualification is on that defendant.

Articles 35 and 36: Appeals and disputes

Article 35 provides a general right of appeal to a magistrates' court against the terms of an Alterations Notice; an Enforcement Notice or a Prohibition Notice (see above). That appeal must be lodged with the magistrates' court by the recipient of the notice within 21 days of receipt of the notice. If an appeal is not lodged within that 21-day deadline, any statutory right of appeal will be lost. However, if an appeal is lodged within the deadline against an Alterations Notice or an Enforcement Notice, the requirements of that notice will be suspended pending the final outcome of that appeal.

That suspension does not apply in the case of a Prohibition Notice, for which immediate compliance may be required unless, on the application of the recipient of the notice, the court directs otherwise.

Following the hearing of an appeal, the magistrates' court can either affirm, cancel, or vary the statutory notice. Article 35(7) provides a further right of appeal (exercisable either by the recipient of the notice or the enforcing authority) to the crown court against an unfavourable decision of the magistrates' court. It must also be assumed that there would also be a right of appeal, but only on a point of law, to the High Court on a case stated.

Article 36 provides an alternative voluntary method of dispute resolution in circumstances where a responsible person has failed to comply with any provisions of the FSO but that person and the enforcing authority cannot agree on what measures are necessary to remedy the failure. In those circumstances, the enforcing authority and the recipient of the notice may agree to refer the outstanding issue to the Secretary of State for determination. Where such a voluntary referral has been made, the Secretary of State may require the timely provision of such further information, including plans, as is needed to make a determination. Once an Article 36 determination has been made, the enforcing authority may not thereafter take any enforcement action which would be in conflict with the Secretary of State's determination. Any Secretary of State determination issued under Article 36 will subsist until any change is made to the premises or its use which changes the risk to relevant persons.

Article 37: Firefighters' switches for luminous tube signs, etc.

Article 37 contains a special provision relating to high-voltage luminous tube signs. Article 37(3) prevents the installation of such apparatus unless it is provided with a regulatory-compliant cut-off switch.

Article 38: Maintenance of facilities and equipment provided for the protection of firefighters

In order to safeguard the safety of firefighters in the event of a fire, the responsible person must ensure that the premises and any facilities, equipment and devices provided to protect firefighters, which are installed to meet any regulatory requirement, are subject to a suitable system of maintenance and are maintained in an efficient state, in efficient working order and in good repair.

Article 39: Civil liability for breach of statutory duty

With one exception, Article 39 makes clear that contravention of the FSO does not confer any automatic right to a civil claim for breach of statutory duty. In that respect the penal provisions contained in the FSO are intended to be entirely self-contained. But this does not mean that an owner or manager of premises cannot be held liable under the general law of negligence for any damage or injury resulting from that person's failure to keep premises safe. There is also a statutory exception preserving the right of employees to sue for any personal injury or other damage resulting from their employer's failure to comply with their responsibilities under the FSO.

Article 40: Employees not to be charged for things done or provided under the FSO

Employers are prohibited from levying any charge against their employees as regards anything done or provided by the employer in compliance with the employer's responsibilities under the FSO.

Article 41: Duty to consult employees

Article 41 extends existing employer consultation requirements contained in the Safety Representatives and Safety Committees Regulations 1977 as well as the Health and Safety Consultation with Employees Regulations 1996 to matters related to the FSO.

Articles 42 and 43: Special provisions for licensed premises

Article 42 relates to premises licensed under any regulatory regime and places the relevant licensing authority as well as the FSO enforcing authority under the following reciprocal requirements:

- A requirement on the licensing authority to ensure that the enforcing authority has the opportunity to make representations before issuing a licence.
- A requirement on the enforcing authority to notify the licensing authority of any action that the enforcing authority takes in relation to premises to which the licence relates.

Article 43 gives the enforcing authority exclusivity as regards the enforcement of the FSO in relation to licensed premises by disapplying the term of any licence which relates to any matter in which requirements or prohibitions could be imposed under the FSO.

Article 44: Suspension of byelaws

To avoid duplication, Article 44 suspends the requirements of any byelaw which relates to any matter for which requirement or prohibitions could be imposed under the FSO.

Article 45: Duty to consult the enforcing authority before passing plans

Article 45 imposes a general duty on local planning authorities to consult the enforcing authority before granting planning permission in relation to any proposal to erect, extend or alter a building, which would otherwise be compliant with building regulations. This requirement to consult also extends to any proposed material change of use of premises to which the FSO relates.

Article 46: Other consultation by public authorities

Article 46 requires any government department or other public authority which intends to take any action in respect of premises which may result in changes for the purposes of the FSO, to first consult the enforcing authority before taking that action.

Article 47: Disapplication of the Health and Safety of Work, etc. Act 1974 in relation to general fire precautions

To avoid duplication and legislative conflict, Article 47 disapplies the Health and Safety at Work etc. Act 1974 as regards premises to which the FSO applies.

Article 48: Service of Notices

Article 48 contains the all-important rules regarding the service of notices under the FSO. If a notice is not correctly served, the notice itself may not be valid. This applies not only to notices served by the enforcing authority but also to any notice served by the responsible person, including any statutory right of appeal to a magistrates' court (which is time-critical). To carry legal validity, an official notice served under the FSO must be addressed to the correct person and to the correct address.

The default position is that any official notice must be delivered as hardcopy. Service by e-mail or facsimile communication will only be deemed valid if the recipient has previously notified the enforcing authority that they will accept as valid, communications which are delivered in that way. Remember also that it is not sufficient just to serve an official notice in the correct way.

Service of that notice may afterwards have to be proved in any subsequent proceedings taken in consequence of that notice.

Article 48(3) states that any official notice served by the enforcing authority must be addressed to the responsible person by name and (if posted) sent to an individual's last known address. In the case of a company, that notice should be addressed to its company secretary at its registered office (even if the particular company does not in fact have a company secretary). The exception is, if, after reasonable enquiry, the name and address of the responsible person cannot be ascertained. The notice may then be served by addressing it to the 'Responsible Person' and by delivering it to some responsible individual who is resident at the premises, or if there is no such person to whom the notice can be delivered, by affixing it or a copy of it to some conspicuous part of the premises.

Article 50 (as amended by Section 2 Fire Safety Act 2021): Official guidance

Article 15 requires the Secretary of State to issue appropriate guidance to assist responsible persons in the discharge of their FSO duties, of which the No 1 Guidance provides an example. Section 3 of the Fire Safety Act 2021 (which adds an additional sub-article 50 (1A)), states that where it is alleged that someone has contravened the FSO, proof of a failure to comply with any applicable risk-based guidance may be relied on as tending to establish that contravention. Equally, proof of compliance with such risk-based guidance may be relied on as tending to establish that there was no such contravention.

Fire Safety (England) Regulations 2022 summarised

The Fire Safety (England) Regulations 2022 were laid before Parliament on 18 May 2022 but do not take effect in England until 23 January 2023, giving building-owners time to prepare for these new legislative requirements. These regulations implement some, but not all, of the recommendations flowing out of Part I Public Inquiry into the 2017 Grenfell fire. They focus on those recommendations regarding the availability of information to fire and rescue services as well as routine safety measures, such as the inspection of lifts, and other key fire-safety equipment, including fire-doors. The regulations do not implement inquiry recommendations for personal emergency evacuation plans (PEEPS), which may be the subject of later regulation.

Here is a summary of the 2022 Regulations:

- *Regulation 3* defines a high-rise building as being either at least 18 metres above ground level or having at least seven storeys.
- *Regulation 4* requires the installation of a secure information box in every high-rise residential building, which must be accessible to the local fire and rescue authority but reasonably secure from unauthorized access and vandalism. The purpose of this box is to contain everything which

firefighters need to know to deal with a fire. The secure information box must contain the name, address and telephone number of the responsible person in the UK as well as contact information for any other persons within the UK who are provided with facilities and permitted to access the building, with such other information as the regulations may require. The responsible person must also provide the local fire and rescue authority with everything required to access the secure information box. The box must be inspected annually to ensure that it remains compliant.

- *Regulation 5* states that the responsible person must, in relation to a high-rise residential building, prepare a record of the design of the external walls of the building, including details of the materials used. That record must include the level of identified risk and any steps taken to mitigate that risk.
- *Regulation 6* requires the responsible person to prepare a plan for each floor. These floor plans must, taken together, identify the location of all lifts and identify which lifts are for use by firefighters or as evacuation lifts as well as the locations of key fire-fighting equipment for the whole building. Where the floor plans for two or more floors are the same, the responsible person has the option of providing a single plan which indicates to which floors it relates. The responsible person must also prepare a single-page building-plan identifying: the environs of the building; how it is used; the dimensions of the building; information as to the number of storeys; information regarding the presence of maisonettes or scissor-section flats; the inlets and outlets for wet and dry mains; location of shut-off controls for sprinklers; access points for the building; location of the secure information box; location of controls for any smoke control systems. A hard copy of the floor plans and building-plan must be placed in the secure information box.
- *Regulation 7* requires the responsible person to undertake monthly routine checks of lifts used by firefighters as well as lifts used for evacuation and essential firefighting equipment. Where an identified fault cannot be rectified within 24 hours, the responsible person must report that fault to the local fire and rescue authority by electronic means. For the purpose of Regulation 7, 'essential firefighting equipment' means the key firefighting equipment (being wet and dry mains, controls for sprinklers and smoke control systems; access points; secure information box) as well as any of the following which are situated within the communal parts of the building: fire-detectors and alarm systems; evacuation alert systems; automatic door release linked to fire-alarm systems. When carrying out routine checks, the responsible person must be satisfied that the equipment is in efficient working order and in good repair in accordance with relevant industry standards and manufacturers' recommendations.
- *Regulation 8* deals with 'wayfinder signage' and requires the responsible person to ensure that there are clear markings as regards floor identification and identification of individual flats. Such markers must be

compliant with building regulations and located within stairways and lift lobbies at each floor level, so as to be visible in low light and also when illuminated by a torch.
- *Regulation 9* deals with the information which responsible persons must give to residents. Note that this requirement to provide information to residents does not only apply to high-rise buildings but to any building containing two or more sets of domestic premises which include common parts which residents would use to evacuate the building in an emergency. Fire-safety information must be in a comprehensible form that residents can reasonably be expected to understand and must include instructions relating to the evacuation strategy for the building and how to report a fire to the fire and rescue authority as well as any other instructions telling residents what to do when a fire has occurred. Note that the requirement to make safety-information comprehensible to residents may involve the need to make that information available in more than one language, according to the demographic make-up of the building. This safety information must be provided to every new resident of the building as soon as reasonably practicable after that resident has moved in. The same information must be provided to existing residents within 12 months from the date these regulations take effect, i.e. before 23 January 2024.
- *Regulation 10* addresses a key recommendation from the Grenfell public inquiry, which stressed the importance of ensuring that fire-doors are fitted with effective self-closing devices and maintained in an operational condition. For any building containing two or more flats and with common parts which residents would have to use to evacuate the building in case of emergency, residents must be informed that fire-doors should be shut when they are not in use and that self-closing devices must not be tampered with. For a residential building above 11 metres in height, the responsible person must use 'best endeavours' to undertake annual checks of fire-doors at the entrances of flats within the building. The use of the words 'best endeavours' acknowledges the fact that a responsible person may be prevented from carrying out an annual fire-door inspection in circumstances where a leaseholder refuses access. The requirement to check the serviceability of fire-doors is increased to three-monthly intervals for those doors situated in communal areas. Each check must ensure that the self-closing device for the particular door is working.
- *Regulation 11* states that in relation to a high-rise residential building, the responsible person must provide the local fire and rescue authority with (Regulation 5) records of the design and materials used in external walls and (Regulation 6) floor plans and building-plan. This information must be provided to the fire and rescue service in an electronic format.

4 PAS 9980:2022 Fire Risk Appraisal of External Wall Construction and Cladding of Existing Blocks of Flats: Code of Practice

Whilst the Fire Safety Order (FSO) provides the regulatory framework for multi-occupied residential buildings and other premises to which the FSO applies, sitting beneath it is a mass of technical guidance intended to cover every situation to which the FSO applies. Whilst such official guidance does not directly have the force of law, the courts will take formal account of such guidance when assessing the extent to which someone has complied – or not complied – with their regulatory responsibilities under the FSO. In particular, it is Article 50 (1A) of the FSO (as inserted by Section 3 of the Fire Safety Act 2021) which states:

> Where in any proceedings it is alleged that a person has contravened a provision of Articles 8 to 22 or regulations made under Article 24 in relation to a relevant building (or part of the building) –
>
> a   proof of a failure to comply with any applicable risk-based guidance may be relied on as tending to establish that there was such a contravention, and
> b   proof of compliance with any applicable risk-based guidance may be relied on as tending to establish that there was no such contravention.

In this chapter we focus specifically on that guidance which is relevant to leaseholders as well as the owners and managers of multi-occupied residential buildings. As with fire-safety law itself, that guidance is always being updated, particularly in the wake of the Grenfell Tower fire. All of the published Fire Safety Act (FSA) guidance which is still current has been collected together on the Home Office website, 'Fire Safety Law and Guidance Documents for Business', which provides links to other official websites. Some of the older guidance, which is still in force but predates the Grenfell fire, must also be approached with caution because it has yet to be updated. The following guidance is of relevance:

1 *Check Your Fire-Safety Responsibilities under the Fire Safety Order* (Home Office, 5 July 2021). This states that the FSO applies to all

DOI: 10.1201/9781003291893-4

workplaces and commercial buildings and the non-domestic parts of multi-occupied residential buildings, including balconies; structures; and the front doors of individual flats. In the case of residential flats, the responsible person is the owner of the non-domestic parts of the building. The guidance then explains that a person has 'control' if they are responsible for the maintenance or repair of the premises or anything in or on the premises or as regards the safety of the premises (for example, a fire-risk assessor, a fire-alarm engineer or managing-agent). Shared premises are likely to have more than one responsible person. For the non-domestic parts, that responsible person is likely to include the landlord, freeholder or managing-agent. There is then the need for those responsible people to coordinate the carrying-out of their responsibilities by sharing information with each other. The guidance defines the requirements of a responsible person as being to undertake a fire-risk assessment which: identifies areas where the fire might start; makes recommendations to reduce the likelihood of fire and keep people safe when a fire happens; and identifies fire-safety measures which are to be taken to make the premises safe for employees or residents as well as for other relevant persons. Whilst there is nothing to prevent a responsible person carrying out a fire-risk assessment directly where they are competent to do so, where someone else is appointed to carry out the task, it is recommended that the appointee has an appropriate accreditation. Currently, in the UK, there are two widely recognised third-party accreditation organisations, namely, the Engineering Council and the UK Accreditation Services.

2   *Fire-Safety in Purpose-Built Blocks of Flats* (Home Office, 2011). This document provides information on how to ensure fire safety in purpose-built blocks of flats and gives practical advice in assessing risk and managing fire safety. Whilst this document must be approached with caution as it reflects the law as it existed in 2011 when first published, this 193-page document provides a wealth of practical advice for the fire safety within such buildings. For the same reason this document can no longer be regarded as 'stand-alone' but must be read together with more recent guidance which has evolved – and which is continuing to evolve – in the wake of the Grenfell fire. That other guidance includes the National Fire Chief Council's Guidance on Simultaneous Evacuation and the PAS 9980: 2022 Code of Practice. In this chapter we scrutinise the latter document.

3   At the time of writing, a proposed guidance note on *Personal Emergency Evacuation Plans* (or PEEPS) is a work-in-process, which is currently the subject of Home Office consultation. The intention of PEEPS is to address the specific fire-safety requirements of residents who have been identified as being likely to have difficulty in self-evacuating from a burning building because of a mobility or other issue relating to their health or well-being. In a high-rise residential building, PEEPS is intended to help provide a targeted approach to evacuation for those residents

in case of fire. Wheelchair users are given as an example. This guidance note will accordingly propose additional legal obligations on a responsible person to prepare a PEEP for every resident who self-identifies as being unable to self-evacuate, and which PEEP is to be made in consultation with that resident. The guidance would also include a PEEP template containing the required information. Key information relating to PEEPS must also be placed in an information box in the building and made accessible to fire and rescue services.

PAS 9980:2022 Fire Risk Appraisal of External Wall Construction and Cladding of Existing Blocks of Flats: Code of Practice

The particular document on which we are going to focus for the remainder of this chapter is the British Standards Institute (2022) publication, *PAS 9980:2022 Fire Risk Appraisal of External Wall Construction and Cladding of Existing Blocks of Flats: Code of Practice* which is abbreviated for the purposes of this chapter to 'the Code'. It is a 180-page stand-alone document commissioned jointly by the newly created Department for Levelling Up, Housing and Communities (which replaced the former Ministry of Housing, Communities and Local Government) and the Home Office. The Code, which took effect on 31 January 2022 and replaced earlier policy guidance, is written primarily as a practice guide for fire-safety engineers, safety engineers and other professionals tasked with advising on the fire-risk of external wall construction of existing blocks of flats. However, it is also intended to be of use to other property professionals who are tasked with making decisions informed by fire-risk appraisals, including: advice agencies; architects; architectural technologists; building owners and landlords (as well as others with legal or functional responsibilities for management of external walls and cladding); building surveyors; contractors; façade engineers; fire and rescue authorities; fire-risk assessors; insurers; local housing authorities; managing-agents or facility managers; project managers; and valuers and mortgage-lenders. The document contains a mass of technical detail as well as policy statements and commentary. As a Code of Practice, PAS 9980:2022 takes the form of recommendations and guidance. It is not to be quoted as a specification.

In this chapter we focus only on the policy statements contained in the first 50 pages of this long document. The complete Code can be downloaded free of charge from the Internet at www.bsigroup.com/en-GB/standards/pas-9980.

PAS 9980 provides guidance on the risk of fire-spread of external wall construction and sets out a methodology to conduct and record fire-risk appraisals of external walls for buildings of varying complexity. It is also to be contrasted with the earlier more risk-averse guidance which it now replaces.

The Code advocates a balanced risk-based approach in which external wall appraisals are only carried out where necessary and not as a matter of routine. Even where such appraisals are deemed necessary, the Code makes the point that not all such appraisals will necessitate intrusive inspection of a building. It is clear that one of the purposes of the Code is to free up scarce resources so that they are targeted only to those buildings necessitating external wall assessment and not to every high-rise residential block. In an introductory note, the British Standards Institute makes the following statements about PAS 9980:2022:

- The carrying out of an assessment using Code methodology does not mean that the building is unsafe.
- The Code is intended for use only by competent professionals and not by lay people.
- It is for use in situations where external wall construction of existing blocks of flats has not been shown to resist fire-spread adequately or where required to inform the fire-risk assessment. Where it is obvious to the fire-risk assessor that the walls don't pose a risk of fire-spread (such as in the case of buildings of traditional brick and masonry construction), there may be no need for a PAS 9980 assessment.
- The Code uses a five-step risk assessment process. It provides a methodology to assist in the identification of risk factors influencing the overall risk rating of a building, as well as mitigation steps that might improve the risk rating.
- The fire-risk posed by external wall construction and cladding is considered to be influenced most by factors falling under the following three broad headings: fire performance; façade configuration; and fire safety/ fire hazards.
- The Code emphasises the importance of proportionality in relation to risk and associated mitigation measures, including considerations of benefit again, practicality and cost.

The phrase used repeatedly throughout the Code is 'fire risk appraisal of external wall construction on existing buildings' which the document has abbreviated to 'FRAEW'. The other abbreviation used throughout the Code is 'FRA', which refers to the regulatory fire risk assessment carried out under the Fire Safety Order (FSO).

Set out below is a summary of the relevant policy statements contained within the Code.

- An FRAEW will not be required in all high-rise or low-rise blocks of flats, particularly where it is manifestly obvious to a competent fire-risk assessor that the risk to life from fire-spread over the external walls is not such as to warrant an FRAEW by a specialist. In these cases the fire-risk assessor will address compliance of external wall construction within the FSO. Fire-risk assessors should therefore be judicious in their recommendations for an FRAEW by a specialist within the action plan of a fire-risk assessment. Unnecessary recommendations for FRAEWs would

- make significant demand on the scarce resources available for FRAEWs, thereby diverting attention from buildings in which the public might be at serious risk and actually do warrant an FRAEW.
- Where an FRAEW is considered necessary, the Code is intended to provide recommendations and guidance tailored to the particular risk posed by the fire spread over the external walls.
- Whilst it is anticipated that the Code will be of interest to a broad readership, its use in a fire-risk appraisal of external wall construction and cladding requires particular skills, knowledge and experience, such that this is a matter for specialists. Users of the Code are asked to consider whether they have the necessary competence before applying the Code recommendations to a particular building.
- Whilst there has been a distinct move towards 'risk-proportionate' fire-safety measures in buildings rather than the more traditional 'prescriptive' approach, concern arising from the Grenfell Tower fire has led some stakeholders to seek a more rigid application of the guidance that supports building regulations, without full consideration of the risk. For those stakeholders the only satisfactory outcome is certainty in the performance of external walls in fire, with zero risk to life as the principal objective. The Code's methodology cannot therefore be applied when such a view prevails.
- The Code's stated objectives are:

  a to provide competent fire engineers and other competent professionals with a methodology for appraising and assessing the scope and the risk from fire-spread via external wall construction and cladding, to inform a building's fire-risk assessment (FRA);

  b to assist external wall assessors in communicating clearly the results of an FRAEW, so recipients can understand the process and methodology applied and understand the findings;

  c to assist other professionals in reviewing an FRAEW and in understanding the risk of external fire-spread in the context of the building's fire strategy and fire-safety arrangements;

  d to promote better understanding of fire risks associated with external walls and the limitations of what can, and cannot, be achieved in any FRAEW in contrast with ensuring conformity of new construction to the standards for new buildings;

  e to enable common relevant terminology to be adopted by those who carry out an FRAEW;

  f to promote consistency in FRAEWs, and to provide a pragmatic and risk-proportionate approach in an FRAEW;

  g to establish a satisfactory basis for documentation of FRAEWs;

  h to enable consistent training in carrying out an FRAEW and thus facilitating more entrants into that profession;

  i to satisfy professional indemnity insurers that there is a national standard that underpins consistency in carrying out FRAEWs.

- The purpose of an FRAEW is to assess the risk to occupants from a fire spreading over or within the external walls of the building and to make a decision as to whether, in the specific circumstances of the building, remediation or other mitigating measures to address the risks are considered necessary. It is applicable where the risk is known, or suspected, to arise from the form of construction used for external wall build-up, such as the presence of combustible materials. The outcome of an FRAEW is intended to inform fire-risk assessments (FRAs) of multi-storey, multi-occupied residential buildings.
- Although the Code applies predominantly to multi-storey blocks of flats, it also includes the following because of their similarity: student accommodation; sheltered or other specialized housing, and buildings converted into flats.
- Before accepting a commission for an FRAEW, the external wall assessor should inform the person commissioning the FRAEW of its inherent limitations, namely, it is intended primarily to inform the building's FRA; it cannot warrant absolute safety as it will be risk-based and therefore reliant on professional judgement by competent persons; it might not be possible to identify the full scope of the works needed as part of the FRAEW from the outset as the conclusion might be that a further inspection or in-depth technical assessment is needed, which might involve the engagement of other professionals; it is not specifically intended to address protection of firefighters; it is not intended to address property protection; and it can only be based on available industry knowledge at the time of the FRAEW.
- Before accepting the commission for an FRAEW, the persons engaged to conduct it should establish that: the building is within the scope of the Code; the purpose of the FRAEW is to inform the building's FRA; a risk-based approach is required and not an unrealistic attempt to establish zero risk; the objective of assessing fire-risk is to address the safety of occupants; and they have the necessary competence to address the risks posed by the particular wall build-ups on the building.
- When adopting a risk-based approach to determine whether an existing block of flats is safe, in terms of external fire-spread, external wall assessors should recognise and take account of: the combustibility and fire performance of external wall construction and cladding; the likelihood of secondary fires; whether a secondary fire is likely to result in direct harm to occupants or prevents them escaping; the role of fire and rescue service intervention, its effectiveness and its limitations; the time it might take for adverse consequences to occur and whether this can be mitigated by, for example, suitable fire design; and the extent and effectiveness of fire-safety management for the building.
- External wall assessors should understand the relationship between the FRAEW and the building's FRA, including the fact that an outcome of an FRAEW could require revision of an FRA dependent on its findings.

- Failure of a building to meet the benchmarks given in regulations and guidance applicable to external wall construction, both currently and at the time when the building was built, should not be used as a sole basis for determining the outcome of the FRAEW.
- The FRAEW should adopt a risk-based approach to include not only the fire behaviour of the materials, components and systems within the external walls, but also other risk factors, such as how the façades are configured on the building, the fire hazards in and around the building and the fire-safety features of the building.
- Assessors should take into account the principle of proportionality when formulating an opinion on the risk and the appropriate mitigation measures in response to that risk, including considerations of benefit gained, practicality and cost.
- Where the FRAEW establishes an immediate risk to life, the assessor should notify the responsible person as soon as possible, giving details of mitigating measures that might be appropriate. It is necessary, if there is an immediate risk to life, there will be significant findings in the FRAEW, and the assessors should recommend a review of the building's FRA, taking into account the FRAEW's findings and recommendations on the necessity for, urgency of, and nature of, interim measures that are considered appropriate.
- In determining the level of risk, assessors should understand the limitations of the fire and rescue service intervention, and avoid over-reliance on such intervention to compensate for adverse features of the external wall construction in relation to its performance in fire.
- Assessors should study, where possible, all original documents relevant to the building's construction and performance in fire and of its FRA. On-site verification should be carried out to establish the veracity of the information, the extent of which shall be determined by the quality and extent of the documentation available. Where the composition of the external walls and methods of construction cannot be established from documentation and initial on-site verification work, the extent of site survey and inspection should be increased accordingly.
- Site surveys and inspections of external walls for an FRAEW should minimise the need for opening-up work and maximise the benefits where such work is required.
- When presented with reports of investigations carried out by others prior to the FRAEW being commissioned, assessors should plan inspections so that it can assist in establishing the veracity of the information they contain to the extent considered necessary.
- Assessors should accurately record their findings in a form suitable for inclusion in an FRAEW report, including plans and photographic evidence where appropriate. The findings should be presented in such a way as to enable persons scrutinising the report to be able to determine: the locations at which opening-up took place and from which samples have

been removed; the identity of samples removed for testing and locations from where they were taken; the nature and extent of deficiencies, deterioration of products and workmanship issues identified, and the locations where they were observed; and differences between what is found in reality and the building's original design.

- When an assessor has identified that combustible material is present, they should then establish the significance of that material on the likely rate of fire-spread, based on an understanding of the quantity of material, its location within the wall build-up and its behaviour in fire.
- The FRAEW should establish, so far as possible, all available indicators of the fire performance of the materials, components and systems forming the external walls of the building.
- The FRAEW should follow a structured approach to determine an outcome with respect to the fire-risk posed by the external wall construction. It should demonstrate that all reasonably practicable efforts have been made to fully determine and take into account: the likely performance of the external walls in a fire; how the fire would start, develop and spread when taking into account all relevant factors relating to the configuration of the cladding, etc., on the façades; and how such a fire could directly, or indirectly, cause harm to the occupants and impact on their ability to escape in time.
- The risk factor should be weighted, according to the relative importance, to determine how significant they are, collectively, in establishing whether relevant benchmark criteria have been met.
- The approach taken should enable a conclusion to be made on whether the external walls of each of the buildings and elevations, or parts of the walls, depending on the configuration of the cladding, present a 'high', 'medium' or 'low' risk and the assessor should highlight where there is potential for further investigation.
- FRAEW reports should make clear that purpose and their relationship to the building's FRA and that it is intended to inform the building's FRA and that its findings are to be interpreted in the context of on-going legislative control over the building under the FSO.
- The report should state clearly that it addresses life safety only in relation to the appraisal of the external walls of the building.
- The report should clearly state that the FRAEW does not confirm compliance with building regulations, either at the time of construction or currently.
- The report should set out, as a minimum: an executive summary giving key findings and overall assessment of the risk rating; a basic factual description of the building, including external wall construction (with drawings or photographs as appropriate); a description of the building in terms of its fire strategy and fire-safety design, to the extent that these can be ascertained; details of the site survey and inspection; the necessity for, urgency of, and nature of any interim measures that are considered

appropriate; and recommendations on remedial action considered necessary, with a suitable time-frame that takes into account both the nature of the works required for remediation and the recommended interim measures. FRAEW reports should contain an explanation of the basis for the outcome and the risk-rating that is deemed to apply, relating back to stated benchmark criteria.

5 Fire safety and leasehold frameworks

A significant problem for many millions of high-rise residential-leaseholders is that although they are the people facing massive service-charge bills to rectify identified fire-risk within their blocks, they are in the hands of another party when it comes to the actions needed to address those issues. That other party is the ground-landlord or management company which is legally responsible for those issues. It is not something which any individual leaseholder can deal with directly and in isolation.

Even where leaseholders are collectively agreed on the need to carry out essential works, there may still be legal obstacles preventing the implementation of those measures, particularly in the face of disinterest by a remote ground-landlord. It is usually only the ground-landlord or building-manager who can commission any works affecting the walls, main structure and communal areas and installations of a building. It is only the ground-landlord or building-manager who can apply for any grant-funding to help assist with the cost of those works. It is only the ground-landlord or building-manager who can put in place the legal steps to ensure that every leaseholder pays their fair share for the cost of remedial works. So what happens when that remote ground-landlord simply doesn't want to know? Or cannot be found?

This will not be an issue for those leaseholders who already collectively manage their own affairs through a freehold management company, in which they each hold a share. But many leaseholders are not in that happy position. Maybe that freehold interest in a block of flats was purchased by someone long ago as an investment. Indeed, until the law changed in 1987, 'ground-rents' could be bought and sold over the heads of leaseholders as easily as stocks and shares. The 'investment value', being primarily the capitalised value of the ground rents, together with the longer-term prospect of being able to sell lease-extensions as individual lease-terms shortened to the extent that they became unattractive to mortgage-lenders. An added bonus was being able to turn a profit from the actual management of a block.

Buying a reversionary-freehold had always been a secure investment as individual leaseholders had no choice but to pay whatever was demanded to avoid their leases becoming forfeit. However, as will be explained later in this chapter, there are now effective remedies available to leaseholders (either

DOI: 10.1201/9781003291893-5

individually or collectively) in circumstances where a remote ground-landlord is refusing to act or who perhaps simply cannot be found. These remedies include the statutory rights which leaseholders now have either to collectively buy out their landlord's interest or simply take over responsibility for management of their block. Even where the statutory eligibility criteria to buy out a freehold or assume direct management responsibility for a block of flats have not been met, there remains the statutory fall-back contained in Part II of the Landlord and Tenant Act 1987, when it can be proved that the ground-landlord is at fault as regards the management of the block. Sections 123–124 of the Building Safety Act 2022 will enable a First Tier Tribunal to issue a Remediation Order requiring a landlord to remedy specified defects to a specified building within a specified time.

Responsibility for fire safety in a multi-occupied residential building cannot be separated from the way in which leases of individual flats within that building are structured. It is that leasehold framework which will determine who is responsible for each individual part of that building. Thus, under a modern residential ground-lease, it is likely to be the ground-landlord or building-manager who is responsible for the foundations, main structure and exterior of the building, all communal areas, including shared utility services, as well as the roof of the building. Individual flat-owners will be responsible for everything which is inside their flats, including utility services which are exclusive to that flat and which are not shared with other flats. For consistency with responsibilities under the Fire Safety Order (FSO), the front doors of each of the flats leading on to the ground floor lobby or landing, should be a landlord responsibility because of their role in preventing the spread of fire within a building. But many older leases are not structured in this way.

The front door of each individual flat leading on to the corridor or hallway should be a self-closing fire-door. If it is not, it will be a fire-risk and will need to be replaced. That door-replacement is easier to manage if the individual leases of the relevant flats reserve ownership of the door to the ground-landlord. In that circumstance it will be easy enough for a ground-landlord to put in hand a comprehensive programme of door-replacement within the building to make it fire-safe and pass on those costs to leaseholders through the annual service-charge. But supposing that door technically forms part of the flat and therefore belongs to the leaseholder? It means that although the landlord will have overall responsibility for fire safety, it may not have the power to insist that front doors are replaced, save where it can be proved that leaseholders are in breach of their own obligations to maintain their front doors in an operational condition.

This is why it is important for anyone tasked with the management of fire safety in a multi-occupied residential building to understand the detailed leasehold structure which governs the legal relationship between that building-manager and every individual leaseholder within that building. Managing fire safety in any multi-occupied residential building is not just about knowing what the

FSO requires the building-manager to do. It is also about knowing what each individual lease *allows* the building-manager to do and, more particularly, what it allows the building-manager to recharge as regards fire-safety management, remediation and improvement.

As a concept, the residential ground-lease may have existed for a 1000 years. But it is only within the past 50 years that it has become the long standardised document which it is today. For example, some older leases include, within their demise, the exterior walls and structure of that part of the building within which the flat is situated. Whereas in a modern purpose-built block of flats, one would expect buildings insurance to be the direct responsibility of the ground-landlord, with the costs being passed back to individual leaseholders through a service-charge, with many older leases, that insurance responsibility is apportioned between individual leaseholders on a flat-by-flat basis, with perhaps different insurance companies insuring different flats.

It must also be remembered that the modern-precedent residential lease presupposes a purpose-built blocks of flats. But what about the many residential conversions, where a large house has been turned into several flats? The leases of those flats are likely to be more bespoke, according to the personal preferences of the conveyancing lawyer who acted for the building-owner at the time of that residential conversion.

Any residential lease also has to conform to the requirements of mainstream lending institutions, so that the property is mortgageable and therefore saleable. It is why there has to be strict reference to the *Mortgage-Lenders Handbook*, now published and updated by UK Finance, which is the representative body for mortgage-lenders within the UK. The fact that an older residential lease is not in strict conformity with the *Handbook* does not necessarily make the property unmortgageable provided that any residual risk to the lending institution resulting from that non-conformity can be covered by title-indemnity insurance.

Our starting point is to analyse the typical structure of a modern lease of an apartment situated within a purpose-built block of flats, which breaks down as follows:

- *The date of the lease.*
- *The names and addresses of the original parties to the lease.* But remember that these details will almost certainly change over the lifetime of the lease with each re-sale of the flat or the landlord-reversion. Therefore, it will always be necessary to check Land Registry records for the most up-to-date information as to the current leaseholder and landlord. As well as the named landlord and the named leaseholder, there may also be a named third-party management company set up to take responsibility for the long-term management of the building and associated amenity areas.
- *The term of the lease.* This can range from 99 years from the date of grant until a virtual-freehold, of 999 years with a modern norm for at least 150 years.

- *The amount of the ground rent.* Traditionally this was always of a nominal amount quickly eroded by inflation, although in recent years some landlords had begun to insist on escalating ground-rents.
- *A description of the property which is leased.* This is perhaps the most crucial part of a typical residential lease as it defines in detail which parts of the apartment 'belong' to the leaseholder and which parts 'belong' to the landlord. Typically, the internal parts of an apartment will belong to the leaseholder whilst the structure and exterior of an apartment will belong to the ground-landlord. So what about that crucial self-closing fire-door, which we have already mentioned and which doubles as the front door of the flat, separating it from the hallway or landing? To whom does that belong? And what about that external balcony? Does that actually 'belong' to the leaseholder? Or does the leaseholder just have the right to use that balcony? These are technical questions which only come to prominence when something has to be repaired or replaced. It depends on how the apartment is described in the lease and what, in particular, is included or excluded.
- *Rights and reservations.* A residential apartment does not exist in isolation. The occupants also need unrestricted access to those apartments via entrance lobbies, stairway, lifts, and landings. They also need access to electricity, water, drainage and related utility services which run through other parts of the building and its grounds. Those occupants may also enjoy use of associated outdoor amenity areas, general car parking, bin-stores, refuse disposal chutes. Maybe even a communal heating system. These communal facilities are often described in leases as 'common parts', and are the direct responsibility of the ground-landlord or management company, with the associated costs being shared between leaseholders through an annual service-charge. As well as granting associated rights to leaseholders, a typical residential lease will also 'reserve' certain rights to the ground-landlord and other leaseholders. This will include shared utility services physically situated within the flat but shared with other leaseholders, such as communal drainage. The landlord might also require access from time to time to carry out its own landlord-responsibilities, particularly as regards the need to access the main structure and exterior of the building, where this cannot conveniently be accessed without entering the apartment.
- *Responsibility for repairs.* A well-drawn-up residential lease will clearly apportion, between the landlord and tenant, the responsibility for repairs and maintenance for every part of the building and its grounds. The leaseholder can only be directly responsible for what is included within the lease, such as the interior of the apartment; non-structural internal walls and partitions; the internal surfaces of the external walls, floors and ceilings; and any utilities which serve the apartment exclusively. Other leaseholders will have similar exclusive responsibility for their own apartments. Everything else relating to the management, repair and maintenance of

the building and its surrounds will be the landlord's or management company's responsibility but with the ability of that landlord or management company to recover its costs from the individual leaseholders through an annual service-charge *provided that the correct procedures have been followed*. More details of those procedures are explained later in this chapter.
- *Insurance.* A modern lease of a residential apartment will generally make the landlord or management company directly responsible for obtaining buildings insurance for the benefit of the building as well as each individual leaseholder and with the cost of insurance being passed back to leaseholders through the annual service-charge (see below).
- *Detailed service-charge provisions.* As well as the nominal ground-rent, residential leaseholders will also be responsible for payment of an annual service-charge to the ground-landlord or management company to cover the actual and projected costs of its maintenance, repairing and management responsibilities. The service-charge provisions between landlord and tenant relate directly back to the apportionment of the repairing responsibilities (between landlord, tenant and management company). In its simplest form, a service-charge might read as nothing more than a single-paragraph obligation on the part of each leaseholder to contribute towards shared costs. But for most modern leases, the particular service-charge items for which each leaseholder is required to contribute is listed out in a service-charge schedule which forms part of the lease. Whilst such service-charge schedules are intended to be comprehensive, they are not fail-safe. It is why the service-charge provisions in most modern residential leases will now include a 'sweeper' clause enabling landlords from time to time to add to recoverable service-charge items to deal with anything which may not have previously been foreseen or to address changing circumstances. *In short, if an item is not listed in the service-charge schedule (either specifically or in general terms), the ground-landlord or management company may have difficulty recovering the cost, if it is recoverable at all.*
- *Restrictions on alterations.* Almost all residential leases of an apartment or maisonette will contain restrictions on what alterations individual leaseholders can carry out within their apartments. The question of any leaseholder carrying out alterations to the structure or exterior should not even arise, as those parts of the building belong to the landlord and not the leaseholder. Even affixing an external satellite dish might then be deemed to be a 'trespass' as that part of the building belongs to the landlord and not the leaseholder. However, most internal alterations will be permissible, provided that the leaseholder has previously obtained the landlord's prior written consent, which under the Landlord and Tenant Act 1927 cannot be unreasonably withheld providing that the leaseholder has agreed to pay the landlord's reasonable costs in considering that request and formally documenting its approval.

- *Restrictions on the way the property can be used.* Obviously, the apartment can be used for residential purposes. But business use may be prohibited. There may be additional restrictions on who can be in occupation at any particular time. Occupation may be restricted to a single household. There may be a prohibition against 'Airbnb' use.
- *Restrictions on sale or subletting.* By its nature, a residential flat has to be freely assignable. If it was not, it wouldn't even be mortgageable. However, some leases may require a formalised landlord consent before the flat can be sold or sub-let, although, under the Landlord and Tenant Act 1988, such landlord consent cannot be unreasonably withheld or delayed, provided that the outgoing leaseholder is prepared to front the landlord's reasonable cost in considering that request and documenting that consent.
- *Compliance with regulatory requirements.* All well-drawn-up residential leases will contain an obligation on the parties to comply with statutory and other regulatory requirements, including town planning legislation. Whether that compliance responsibility falls (in any case) directly on the leaseholder or the ground-landlord or management company depends generally to which part of the building the regulatory provision applies. If it is a 'landlord's part', such as the main structure or a communal area, compliance will be the direct responsibility of the ground-landlord or management company, subject to its right to reimbursement through leasehold service-charges. If it forms part of an individual apartment, such as an internal installation, direct responsibility will rest with the named leaseholder of that apartment. The distinction is perhaps most acute when it comes to the front doors of individual flats leading on to lobbies and landings. Modern fire-safety guidance states that such doors should be fire-safety doors and self-closing. However, whilst primary responsibility for fire safety within a multi-occupied residential building may rest with the ground-landlord or building-manager, changing or repairing a defective fire-door may not be within its direct control.
- *Rules governing behaviour.* The modern residential lease is likely to contain a raft of detailed provisions governing the behaviour of individual leaseholders. These may commonly cover such things as prohibitions on the keeping of pets. Or using a television or other audio-equipment at such a volume as to cause annoyance to other residents. Modern residential leases may also include a 'sweeper' clause, which enables a ground-landlord or management company to make additional regulations, over and above those listed in the lease, dealing with behavioural and related occupancy issues. Such additional regulations may be changed or added to from time to time by the building-manager to the extent that the law would regard them as 'reasonable' and are not in any way inconsistent with the express terms and conditions of the particular lease. *It is suggested that the ability to make supplemental management regulations could be used by building-managers to address on-going fire-safety*

issues requiring minor changes in leaseholder behaviour, such as prohibiting the accumulation of rubbish or the use of any naked flame on an external balcony, where it could present a fire-risk.
- *Landlord obligations*. As well as a long list of leaseholder obligations, there is also a much shorter list of landlord's obligations, which are intended to dovetail in to the overall leasehold structure. This will include the traditional 'covenant for quiet enjoyment', where the landlord agrees to leave the leaseholder in peace to the extent that the leaseholder complies with their own obligations under the lease. More importantly, the landlord obligations must include an obligation to adequately insure the building and maintain the main structure, exterior, foundations, roof and communal parts of the building as well as any outside amenity areas associated with the building, the cost of which will later be shared between individual leaseholders through the annual service-charge.
- *Default provisions*. For its terms to be mutually enforceable by landlords against leaseholders, or vice versa, or between individual leaseholders and other leaseholders, any lease must contain robust provisions enabling such provisions to be enforced against a defaulting party. The traditional 'forfeiture clause' has, for many centuries, been a feature of any well-drawn-up lease and the substance of its wording has barely changed in those centuries. Typically, a forfeiture clause only goes one-way and gives the landlord the right to enter an apartment and evict a leaseholder for any breach of the leaseholders' obligations, even if the ground-rent is as little as 21 days in arrears. Without additional statutory protection, the position of any leaseholder would be precarious, as would be the security of any mortgage-lender. In practice, the position of a residential leaseholder and mortgage-lenders are little more secure. A landlord can never evict a residential-leaseholder without first obtaining a court order, and only then, as a last resort, if it becomes clear that the leaseholder either does not intend to or does not have the ability to comply with the terms of their lease. Another tool in the landlord's armoury is the *Jervis v Harris* clause which is found in most modern residential leases. Named after the 1995 court decision, a *Jervis v Harris* clause is intended to circumvent the Leasehold Property (Repairs) Act 1938 (see below) and provides landlords with a swift summary remedy for dealing with minor repair issues which, if not quickly remedied, could cause a greater problem for the ground-landlords or other leaseholders. Under a *Jervis v Harris* clause, a ground-landlord reserves the right to enter individual apartments at any time, on reasonable notice, for the purpose of making an inventory of outstanding repairs which the leaseholder has failed to carry out. The landlord will then serve that inventory on the individual leaseholder giving them – say – two months to carry out and complete the outstanding items of disrepair, failing which, the landlord can enter the apartment with its own contractors and make good those repairs at the leaseholder's expense.

However, it is important to note that, largely as a result of statutory intervention, the terms of a long residential lease are no longer stand-alone but sit within a wider system of leasehold law designed to protect residential leaseholders against unfair landlord practices and to ensure that leaseholders are kept informed and properly consulted as regards any proposed capital works, such as the removal and/or replacement of defective cladding, considered likely to add substantially to leaseholder service-charges.

Some of those leaseholder protections have evolved over centuries, such as the common-law right of a leaseholder to apply to the court for 'relief against forfeiture', in circumstances where the leaseholder has made good the default and reimbursed the landlord's costs arising out of that default. The grant of such relief will generally be automatic once the default has been made good and the landlord's out-of-pocket expenditure reimbursed. Then there is the Leasehold Property (Repairs) Act 1938 (see above), which restricts the landlord's right to take any legal step to enforce a leaseholder's obligation to repair, by requiring the landlord to first give notice to the leaseholder under the 1938 Act and then giving that leaseholder the ability to serve a counter-notice within 28 days, claiming the protection of the 1938 Act. If the leaseholder serves that counter-notice, the landlord is then prevented from taking any enforcement action in relation to that particular item of disrepair without first having obtained the leave of the court, which can only be granted on one of several limited grounds specified in the 1938 Act.

For all leases (both residential and commercial), the first formal step for any ground-landlord seeking to exercise a right of forfeiture, is service of a notice of intended forfeiture under Section 146 Law of Property Act 1925, giving the leaseholder the last chance to remedy the breach before the lease becomes forfeit. It is a wake-up call. If the leaseholder promptly puts right the outstanding breach (if it is capable of remedy) and reimburses the landlord's out-of-pocket expenditure, that is the end of the matter. If not, the landlord can move on to the next step in the forfeiture process. Note that service of a Section 146 notices is not required where the grounds for repossession are based only on outstanding rent arrears. Though a Section 146 notice will be required for service-charge arrears, unless the terms of the lease deem service-charges to be part of the reserved rent, in which case the need for a prior Section 146 notice may arguably not apply. Note also that for residential leases, the right of a ground-landlord to serve a Section 146 notice in relation to any perceived leaseholder breach is not immediate, but requires the landlord first to have evidenced that breach by a court judgment or decision of a First-Tier Tribunal (see below).

It is Section 2 of the Protection from Eviction Act 1977 which prevents a ground-landlord from exercising any right of forfeiture under a residential lease without first obtaining a court order to do so.

However, the most significant legislation protecting leaseholders from unfair service-charge bills relating to capital works, including those resulting from the removal of flammable cladding, is that contained in the Landlord and Tenant Act 1985, which, with its associated regulations, creates a statutory code for the recovery of service-charges. Here is a summary of its most important provisions.

We begin with Section 19 Landlord and Tenant Act 1985 (limitation of service-charges reasonableness,) which establishes the overarching principle that relevant costs are only to be taken into account in determining the amount of service-charges to the extent that they are reasonably incurred in the provision of services or the carrying-out of works and only if those works or services are of a reasonable standard.

Leaseholder Consultation on Service-Charges

Of more practical significance to residential-leaseholders is Section 20 of the 1985 Act (Limitation of Service Charges – Consultation Requirements), which requires leaseholders to be formally consulted before major works are commissioned or the landlord enters into any long-term contract with a third party which, in either case, will significantly add to the service-charge bills for individual leaseholders. Section 20 also enables the Secretary of State to make detailed regulations governing the process of statutory consultation. Those detailed regulations are currently contained in the Service Charge (Consultation Requirements) (England) Regulations 2003 (which we have abbreviated in this chapter to 'the service-charge regulations').

The first formal indication leaseholders receive that major works are about to be carried out to a building is when the ground-landlord issues a 'Section 20 Notice' stating in general terms the nature of the works which the landlord intends to commission (or in relation to a qualifying long-term agreement which the landlord proposes to enter into) and inviting comment. At that initial stage it is only about the general principle of the proposed works which are to be commissioned. No contract for the carrying-out of the works will actually have been tendered at that stage.

The service-charge regulations contain four schedules differentiating between the types of consultation which need to be carried out, depending on the circumstances of the individual case. Two of the schedules relate to 'qualifying long-term agreements', which are usually agreements to be entered into with a contractor and relating to the general management of a block or on-going maintenance, where the intended duration of that agreement is more than 12 months. Conceivably, such an agreement could encompass on-going fire-safety arrangements. The remaining two schedules, relate to 'qualifying works', such as the stripping-out of defective cladding, which is likely to significantly add to service-charge bills.

Save where the ground-landlord is a public-sector body which is legally required to put all of its contracts out to tender, these service-charge regulations also give leaseholders a collective right to nominate a contractor of their own choice from which the landlord is then obliged to seek a quotation.

Note that the service-charge regulations are only about consultation. A ground-landlord is under no obligation to award the contract to the leaseholders' nominee nor to the cheapest quote. Neither is the ground-landlord at that initial stage committed to commissioning any works at all. The landlord's only obligation is to take sufficient account of and, if required, respond to representations received from leaseholders either individually or collectively.

Having received and taken account of the leaseholders' representations as regards the principle of the work, together with details of any nominee contractor collectively provided by those leaseholders, the second stage in the process is for the ground-landlord to actually put the works out to tender.

Failure to comply with the service-charge regulations means that a ground-landlord may be prevented from charging any individual leaseholder more than £250 for one-off qualifying works or £100 per year for a qualifying long-term agreement. The landlord would then have to meet any excess out its own pocket.

One of the problems with statutory service-charge consultation is that it is complex and time-consuming. However, building-managers may not have the luxury of time when it comes to addressing an urgent fire-safety issue requiring significant capital expenditure. It is why, to address cladding issues, many building-managers elect, instead, to apply directly to the First Tier Tribunal (FTT) under Section 20ZA of the 1985 Act, as amended by later legislation, for an order to dispense with the statutory consultation-requirement which would otherwise be required to recharge this cost to individual leaseholders. Application to an FTT for an order dispensing with consultation-requirements can be made either before the works have been commissioned or retrospectively after the bill has arrived. Grounds for a landlord applying under Section 20ZA for an order dispensing with statutory consultation requirements might be:

- to carry out emergency works (for example, to remove an imminent fire-risk);
- the landlord simply forgot to consult or did not consult adequately;
- it had previously been thought mistakenly that the cost would not have exceeded the statutory threshold of £250 per flat (for qualifying works) but the actual cost was significantly higher.

It is also clear from the Supreme Court's 2013 decision in *Daejan Investments Ltd v Benson and Ors* [2–13] UKSC 14, that FTTs are required to approach landlords' applications under Section 20ZA pragmatically and to grant dispensations in circumstances where the leaseholders did not suffer financial detriment as a result of the landlord's failure to consult. The purpose of Section 20 and its associated regulations is not to punish landlords for any technical non-compliance but to ensure that leaseholders are placed substantially in the same financial position as if the appropriate consultation had been carried out.

A useful starting-point for anyone seeking an understanding of residential leasehold service-charges, particularly as regards fire safety, is the RICS (Royal

Institution of Chartered Surveyors) *Code of Practice: Service-Charge Residential Management Code and Additional Advice to Landlords Leaseholders and Agents* 3rd edition, 1 June 2016, which is freely downloadable at www.rics.org/uk/up holding-professional-standards/. The code is approved by the Secretary of State under Section 87(7) Leasehold Reform, Housing and Urban Development Act 1993 and was prepared to promote desirable practices in relation to the management of residential leasehold property. The stated core principles of the Code are:

- To improve general standards and promote best practice, uniformity, reasonableness and transparency in the management and administration of a long leasehold residential property.
- To ensure the timely issue of all documentation, including budgets and year-end accounts.
- To reduce the causes of disputes and give guidance for resolving disputes where these do occur.

Best practice accordingly requires services to be procured on an appropriate value-for-money basis and that competitive quotations are obtained or costs are benchmarked. All costs should be transparent so that all parties, owners, leaseholders and managing agents are aware of how the costs are made up. The code applies only to residential leasehold properties in England and covers flats, houses and all other dwellings, whether in towns or in the country, on estates, in groups or on their own. It covers leases of any length as well as statutory tenancies where variable service-charges are payable. But note that the Code does not apply where the landlord is a public-sector authority or a registered social landlord. Most importantly, for the purposes of this chapter, the Code contains the following detailed provisions which are relevant to fire-safety.

Section 8.4 of the Code deals with fire-risk assessments and includes the following statement:

> You should ensure that you are familiar with the publications and wider guidance from the HSE (Health and Safety Executive) on fire-risk assessments and management plans. Any works required to fulfil the action plan should be planned with your client without delay. To ascertain if costs are recoverable as a service charge, you should refer to the lease. Where service charge monies are insufficient to meet the expenditure required, you should consult with your client regarding long-term planning or arranging other funding options. Health and safety should not be compromised due to lack of funds and further advice should be taken if necessary. It is essential that escape routes, and the means provided to ensure that they are used safely, are managed and maintained to ensure that they remain usable and available at all times. You should monitor compliance and, if necessary, arrange for items to be removed.

Where necessary, consideration should be given to taking action against leaseholders breaching the terms of their lease. You should have regular testing and servicing arrangements in place for any fire-fighting and detection equipment.

Under the heading 'Emergencies and escalation of works', Section 9.13 of the Code states:

The consultation regulations do not provide any exceptions from the procedures due to urgency. Even if you believe that the works are urgently required, non-compliance with the regulations may lead to any costs in excess of the statutory limit for each leaseholder being irrecoverable. Under Section 20ZA of the Landlord and Tenant Act 1985 the FTT can, however, dispense with or any of the requirements, if satisfied that it is reasonable to do so. If works are urgently required that are likely to exceed the consultation threshold, you should advise your client to seek dispensation from the FTT if a client wishes to recover the full cost of the works as service-charge. In extremely urgent situations your clients may wish to undertake works prior to obtaining dispensation from the FTT, which can be granted retrospectively. Such situations have resulted in a number of challenges in the FTT, but one common theme from resulting determinations is that landlords should undertake as much of the consultation-process as possible. They should attempt to ensure that leaseholders are not prejudiced and the demonstrable value for money has been obtained. The FTT will look at every individual application on its merits, so you should not assume that dispensation will be granted. Dispensation is unlikely to be forthcoming where consultation has not occurred due to incompetence, ignorance or lack of forward planning. Before instructing any contractor to undertake works at the cost above the consultation threshold and without fulfilling all of the statutory consultation-requirements, you should make your client fully aware of all the financial risks involved and only proceed with the client's express instructions to do so. It is not uncommon for contracts to be specified, tendered and works commenced, only to subsequently discover that more extensive works are required at greater cost. This may lead to further consultation being required. It can frequently be prudent or more cost effective to complete the required works, rather than suspending the contract until the consultation-requirements can be fulfilled. This is another situation in which a request can be made to the FTT to grant dispensation from the further consultation-requirement so that the works can continue in a timely manner. The FTT will consider carefully the circumstances of each individual case in deciding if the consultation-requirements have been fully met and, if not, whether to grant dispensation. This is a complex area of case-law and tribunal determinations, with which you should familiarise yourself and take further advice where necessary.

As well as the Service Charge Code set out in the Landlord and Tenant Act 1985, Section 81 of the Housing Act 1996 (as amended) provides leaseholders facing service-charge issues with an additional statutory protection. Under the heading 'Restriction on termination of tenancy for failure to pay a service charge', Section 81(1) states that the landlord may not, in relation to premises let as a dwelling, exercise a right of re-entry or forfeiture for failure by the tenant to pay a service charge, or administration charge, unless either it is finally determined by (or on appeal from) the appropriate tribunal (meaning an FTT, see above) or by a court or by an arbitral tribunal in proceedings pursuant to a post-dispute arbitration agreement that the amount of the service-charge or administration charge is payable by that leaseholder or that the leaseholder has admitted that it is so payable. Once that final decision or admission has been made, a further 14 days must then elapse before the landlord can take any formal step towards forfeiture of the lease.

Section 81(4a) further makes clear that the required FTT decision, court judgment or arbitrator-decision, or formal admission, is needed before the landlord can even serve notice of intended forfeiture under Section 146 Law of Property Act 1925 (see above).

So there is a graduated process to be followed by a landlord in order to exercise a right of forfeiture, which will include: proceedings before a court or FTT to establish the amount of service-charge which is due; service of formal notice of intended forfeiture under Section 146 Law of Property Act 1925; and further proceedings before the court to obtain an order for possession.

What this means is that whilst the forfeiture of a long residential lease because of service-charge arrears is rare, it is not impossible. Many such forfeiture cases have occurred when leaseholders have gone abroad for long periods of time, leaving the flat unoccupied and with no arrangements in place for the forwarding of post or for the payment of service-charges whilst they are away. That absent leaseholder might not then have even been alerted to pending forfeiture proceedings and may return after several years to discover a new family living in their flat.

Although many leases and other commercial agreements contain provisions requiring any dispute to be referred to an independent arbitrator for determination under the Arbitration Act 1996, Section 81 of the Housing Act 1996 refers in specific terms to a 'post-dispute arbitration agreement'. What this means is that any earlier contractual arrangement requiring a referral of disputes to arbitration will not be binding for the purposes of Section 81 unless, after the service-charge dispute has arisen, the parties to that dispute have agreed to that arbitrator's appointment and to be bound by that arbitrator decision.

The other party which will be caught up in any service-charge dispute between landlord and leaseholder will be any mortgagee, whose own financial security will be at risk when a leaseholder is in default under the terms of their lease. In those circumstances, that mortgage-lender may itself elect to step in and pay the outstanding service-charges (even if disputed), which will then be added to the mortgage debt. That is of course assuming that the mortgage-lender is alerted to the situation in sufficient time to protect its financial stake in the property.

Some modern residential leases place landlords under an express contractual obligation to alert known mortgagees before taking any first formal step towards forfeiture of that lease. In any event, the likelihood is that the mortgagee would be alerted at some stage of the repossession-process, which would ordinarily require a court order before it can take effect.

It must also be remembered that leasehold obligations run both ways. Whilst the primary obligation is on the leaseholder to pay the ground-rent and associated service-charges as well as complying with management regulations, there are also obligations on a ground-landlord to insure the building and maintain the structure and exterior as well as the communal parts of the building and its surroundings. What is different is the way those respective contractual obligations can be enforced.

Onerous forfeiture provisions are only related to non-compliance of leaseholder obligations. However, there is no corresponding provision for the forfeiture of a landlord's interest, even where that breach is so serious as to put the safety of leaseholders at risk. In short, the contractual mechanisms for enforcing landlord obligations within a long residential lease are weak compared with the onerous remedies which are available to a landlord in the event of non-compliance by leaseholders of their contractual obligations. Without statutory intervention the position of leaseholders might be impossible in circumstances where a ground-landlord is dilatory as regards performance of its landlord obligations or, worse still, abandons those obligations altogether.

It is that statutory intervention which now gives leaseholders, faced with that situation, the collective ability to take over the active day-to-day maintenance and management of their buildings. The value of the landlord's interest in the building is still protected, but that landlord will no longer have the ability to delay or frustrate the carrying-out of essential works, including those related to fire safety. A summary of the most relevant statutory provisions giving leaseholders the collective ability to take over the management of their blocks is set out below:

The Landlord and Tenant Act 1987 contains the following fault-based remedies to collectively assist leaseholders when faced with a ground-landlord which is either not adequately fulfilling obligations related to the essential maintenance or insurance of a residential-building, or which has abandoned those obligations altogether.

Part II of the 1987 Act enables any leaseholder or group of leaseholders to apply to a First Tier Tribunal to appoint a manager to carry out those landlord functions on proof that the landlord is in breach of an obligation owed to leaseholders relating to the management of the premises but only to the extent that it is just and convenient to make an appointment. Such an order can also be made where a ground-landlord has made or proposed unreasonable service or administration charges; or has failed to comply with any relevant provision of a code of practice approved by the Secretary of State under Section 87 Leasehold Reform Housing and Urban Development Act 1993 (codes of management practice) or that other grounds exist for making such an appointment. Again the First Tier Tribunal (FTT) must be satisfied that it is just and convenient to make that appointment. Section 110 of the Building Safety Act 2022 states that the FTT's power to appoint a manager does not apply in respect of a breach of a Building Safety Obligation by an Accountable Person for a higher-risk building. Nor may an order provide for a manager to carry out a function in relation to a higher-risk building where Part 4 of that Act or associated regulations provide for that function to be carried out by an Accountable Person.

In circumstances where an FTT has appointed a manager under Part II of the 1987 Act and that appointment has remained in force for at least two years, leaseholders can collectively apply to the court under Part III of the 1987 Act for an order enabling someone nominated by those leaseholders to buy out the landlord's interest. In other words it takes the form of a compulsory acquisition by the leaseholders of the landlord's interest in the building. However, that order can only be made on proof that the landlord is in breach of obligations owed to the applicants relating to the management of the premises and that the same breach is likely to continue.

Where compulsory acquisition of a landlord's interest differs from a landlord's right to forfeit a lease where a tenant is in breach, is that under the Part III provisions, the ground-landlord is paid full value for its acquired interest.

Part IV of the 1987 Act deals with the situation where a residential lease fails to deal adequately with the maintenance and insurance of a block of flats. In those circumstances either the ground-landlord or any leaseholder can apply to a First-Tier Tribunal for an order to amend the terms of existing leases so as to adequately deal with such matters.

Part I of the Leasehold Reform Housing and Urban Development Act 1993 gives leaseholders a collective right to buy out a ground-landlord's interest, effectively making those leaseholders their own landlord. The landlord and tenant functions otherwise remain separate within the terms of those individual leases. The enfranchisement process does not require proof of any fault on the part of the out-going landlord but requires participation by a majority of the 'qualifying' leaseholders within the building. In general, a lease will be 'qualifying' if originally granted for a term in excess of 21 years and only so long as none of the handful of statutory exemptions apply. Again, the ground-landlord is paid full market value for its interest in the building.

Part 2, Chapter 1 of the Commonhold and Leasehold Reform Act 2002 introduced a new non-fault 'right to manage', providing an administrative process by which leaseholders can collectively take over from their ground-landlord responsibility for the repair, maintenance, insurance and management of their blocks. Again, a majority of qualifying leaseholders need to participate to exercise the right. There is also a requirement on those leaseholders to exercise management through a dedicated 'right to manage' company, for which model articles of association are provided. Unlike freehold enfranchisement, there is no buying-out of the landlord's interest and, for that reason, it might be considered a cheaper option.

Note the prospective amendment to the service-charge regime contained in Section 133 of the Building Safety Act 2022 and which introduces a new Section 20D (limitation of service-charges: remediation works), into the Landlord and Tenant Act 1985, which will require landlords to take reasonable steps to ascertain whether any grant is payable in relation to remediation works, and, if so, to obtain that grant. Also for the landlord to take reasonable steps to ascertain whether money may be obtained from a third party in connection with the undertaking of the remediation works and to obtain monies from that third party. This might include third-party funds from a policy of insurance or under a guarantee or indemnity or pursuant to a claim against a developer or anyone involved in the design of the works or in carrying out those works. Schedule 8 of the Building Safety Act 2022 will further limit recovery of remediation costs in relation to 'qualifying leases'. A lease is a 'qualifying' lease if is for more than 21 years; was granted before 14 February 2022 and was the tenant's only or principal home. A defect is 'relevant' if it arose as a result of something done or not done and relates to a Building Safety Risk.

In the final part of this chapter we address some specific situations relating to leasehold structures which are relevant to the fire safety of a residential building.

Leaseholders are collectively their own landlord

This might be because the leaseholders have previously exercised a statutory right of collective enfranchise (see above) or as a result of some other contractual arrangement. It also covers the half-way situation where leaseholders do not collectively own their freehold but instead have taken over statutory responsibility for the management of a block. In either of those situations, the leaseholders are directly and collectively responsible for the implementation of all required fire-safety measures within that building. Simply because there is no-one else to whom that responsibility can be passed back.

However, as previously stated, there remains separation between the landlord and tenant obligations in relation to each of those individual leases. Acting collectively, the leaseholders are directly responsible for the insurance of the building as well as the repair and maintenance of the foundations, main structure, exterior, roof and all communal parts of the building and its surrounds. Acting collectively, leaseholders must also comply with the technical requirements for the levying of service-charges, as set out in the Landlord and Tenant Act 1985, otherwise those service-charges may not be enforceable against individual leaseholders, which means that everyone else will need to make up the shortfall.

For larger blocks of flats, it is likely that the leaseholders will collectively exercise their landlord function through a dedicated freehold management company, in which each of the participating leaseholders enjoys equal voting rights. Whilst there is currently no statutory obligation on leaseholders to collectively operate through a management company, we would regard it as preferable that the landlord function is exercised in this way as it provides continuity and also enables decisions to be made on a majority vote. The mandatory setting-up of a company currently only applies to exercise of the statutory no-fault right to manage under Part 2 of the 2002 Act. Section 111 of the Building Safety Act 2022 will insert an implied provision in the Articles of Association of a residents' managing company relating to the appointment of a Building Safety Director. Whilst the Building Safety Director can be appointed from amongst the leaseholders themselves, it is intended to be a professional paid position, the remuneration for which can be included in the annual service charge,

Flats above shops or other commercial premises

The position is different again for flats which are built above commercial premises. For a start, the extensive statutory leaseholder protections which apply to residential-leases have no application to shop and other commercial lettings, which are more likely to be shorter and at the full market rent.

The general legislation applying to commercial lettings is Part II of the Landlord and Tenant Act 1954 which, with some tweaks, has barely changed since it was originally enacted. What this means is that there are two mutually exclusive systems of leasehold-tenure existing within the same building. However, in practice, the responsibility for statutory fire safety will in most cases rest with the same landlord or building-manager. If the commercial element comprises more than 25 per cent of the building as a whole, this may prevent leaseholders collectively exercising their right to buy out their freehold. But it should not prevent leaseholders applying to a First Tier Tribunal under the 1987 Act for the appointment of a manager where the leaseholders' interests are at risk because of landlord failures.

Building Safety Act 2022 – Prospective Amendments – Implied Terms Relating to Building Safety and Building Safety Charge

Our starting point has to be Section 113 of the Act, which will insert a new Section 47A into the Landlord and Tenant Act 1987, requiring Building Safety Information to be included in rent demands relating to a higher-risk building. That information to include the fact that it is a higher-risk building; the name and contact details of the principal Accountable Person and any Special Measures Manager; and the regulator's postal address. When it becomes law, Section 112 of the Act will insert a new Section 30C into the Landlord and Tenant Act 1985, which will apply to any lease of premises which consists of or includes a dwelling in a higher-risk building. In each such lease there will be implied a warranty on the part of the landlord to comply with their building safety duties; to co-operate with other responsible persons in complying with their building safety duties and, where there is in force a Special Measures Order, to comply with that Order so far as it relates to the landlord. There is further a reciprocal implied covenant by the leaseholder to allow the landlord, a relevant person or other authorised person, to enter their premises for a relevant Building Safety Purpose and, where a Special Measures Order is in force, to comply with that order so far as it relates to the leaseholder.

Special Measures Orders are addressed in Section 102 and Schedule 7 of the Act and enable the Regulator to apply to a First-Tier Tribunal for an order appointing someone to be a 'special measures manager' for a building to carry out building-safety functions and to collect Building Safety Charges (see below). The grounds for such an order are that there has been a serious failure, or failure on two or more occasions, by an accountable person for the building to comply with a regulatory duty.

The Act also supplements the existing Part IV of the Landlord and Tenant Act 1987 by introducing a new Section 24ZA (application for appointment of a manager by a special measures manager).

A further implied term relating to building safety costs will also be introduced by a new clause 30D in the 1985 Act which will enable landlords to levy against leaseholders 'Building Safety Costs' to cover costs or estimated costs to be incurred by an accountable person or special measures manager for a higher-risk building in connection with taking building safety measures. Building safety costs primarily cover the administrative costs related to fire safety. They cannot cover the cost of capital works to remedy the fire-risk, which will be dealt with in accordance with the general 1985 Act service-charge regime.

Safety measures which can be taken into account in calculating building safety costs are: applying for registration; applying for a building assessment certificate and displaying the same; appointing a building-safety manager; assessing building safety risks; taking reasonable steps to manage building safety risks; preparing and revising a safety case report and notifying the same to the regulator; establishing and operating a mandatory occurrence reporting system and providing information to the regulator; keeping information and documents and supplying the same; preparing, reviewing and revising a residents' engagement strategy and providing copies of that strategy to residents; establishing and operating a system for the investigation of complaints; giving a contravention notice to residents and making application to the county court; and making a request to enter premises.

6 The Defective Premises Act 1972 (DPA) (as amended)

The best mutual outcome for leaseholders and building-managers facing expensive fire-remediation works is to be able to pass that responsibility and liability back to a third party. That third party might be the organisation responsible for the installation of defective cladding or by giving approval for that installation. Or there could be an opportunity to obtain grant funding to pick up part of that cost, so that it does not all translate into service-charges.

The Defective Premises Act 1972 (DPA) was introduced to plug a gap in the law, which hitherto had meant that landlords were not responsible for the state or condition in which premises were let, even if someone suffered injury as a result. The terms of the 1972 Act are now summarised as follows.

Under the heading 'Duty to build dwellings properly', Section 1 of the Defective Premises Act 1972 (DPA) states that anyone taking on work to provide a dwelling, including conversion or enlargement of an existing building, owes a duty to see that the work undertaken is done in a workmanlike and professional manner and with proper materials so that, as regards that particular work, the dwelling will be fit for habitation when completed. That duty is owed to the person who commissioned the work as well as to every person who, going forward, acquires an interest in the dwelling. It doesn't matter if a house-builder sub-contracted part of the construction, they will still be liable for the finished product.

The weakness in this statutory obligation is that it is time-limited. Unless proceedings for breach of the duty is brought within the six-year time limit prescribed by the Limitation Act 1980, any claim under the Act for defective construction will be time-barred. Note, however, that the six-year time-limitation may begin to run afresh in circumstances where further work is carried out to rectify defective work which had previously been carried out (Section 5 DPA). Note also a prospective amendment contained within Section 135 of the Building Safety Act 2022 which will introduce a new Section 4A to the Limitation Act 1980 which will extend from 6 years to 15 years the time limit for bringing claims under the DPA as well as Section 38 of the Building Act 1984 [civil liability for breach of Building Regulations]. That 15-year limitation period extends to up to 30 years for defective building work which was completed before these legislative provisions came into force.

DOI: 10.1201/9781003291893-6

To avoid duplication, Section 2 of the DPA excludes liability in circumstances where the first buyer of a completed dwelling benefits from an 'approved scheme' such as that offered by the National House Building Council (NHBC), which will offer better contractual protection lasting up to 10 years.

When it comes into force, the Building Safety Act 2022 will also amend the DPA by introducing a new Section 2A which will apply when someone in the course of a business takes on work in relation to a building consisting of one or more dwellings. Where the new Section 2A applies, the person carrying out the work will owe a duty not only to the person by whom the work is done but also to anyone who holds or acquires an interest in any dwelling in the building, to see that the work is done in a workmanlike and professional manner, and with proper materials so that, as regards the work, the dwelling is fit for habitation when the work is completed.

Section 3 of the DPA makes clear that the house-builder is not absolved of liability as a result of any future on-going sale of the dwelling to a third party. It is then that third party who will also have the right to claim against the original house-builder for defective work alongside the original purchaser.

In contrast to the earlier time-limited provisions, Section 4 places an on-going 'Landlord's duty of care in virtue of an obligation or right to repair premises demised'. This means that where premises are let under a tenancy placing the landlord under an obligation to maintain or repair the premises, the landlord owes a duty to everyone who might reasonably be expected to be affected by defects in the state of the premises, to see that they are reasonably safe from personal injury or from damage to property caused by the relevant defect. That duty is owed if, in all the circumstances of the case, the landlord knows or ought to have known of a relevant defect. A defect is 'relevant' if it existed at the beginning or subsequent to the start of the tenancy and arose from an act or omission of the landlord which constituted a failure to carry out an obligation to the tenant as regards the maintenance or repair of the premises.

For short-term residential lettings of less than seven years, Section 11 of the Landlord and Tenant Act 1985 puts landlords under a non-negotiable obligation to maintain the structure, exterior and main installations of a dwelling which is let. For a flat which is let under a long residential lease, that landlord obligation is likely to be found within the terms of the lease itself. A modern well-drawn residential lease will place the ground-landlord under an express obligation to maintain the foundations, main structure, exterior, roof and communal parts of a building and its surrounds. But a ground-landlord's obligation under Section 4 of the DPA will not absolve those leaseholders from their obligation to contribute towards the landlord's costs in complying with that duty, save to the extent that those costs can be unloaded onto a third party.

The limited extent to which the DPA can assist leaseholders faced with the costs of replacing flammable cladding was highlighted in the recent case of *SportCity v Countryside Properties (UK) Limited*, [2020] EWHC 1591

(TCC), when it was held that three leasehold management companies were timed-out for bringing claims under the DPA in respect of defective cladding, where the original development was completed by 2010 but the development company ('Countryside') returned in 2014 to carry out further work in relation to the cladding, following complaints a year earlier that there were problems with that cladding. The leasehold structure was itself complex.

Manchester City Council is the freehold owner of the land on which the complex was built. It sold the land on three 250-year leases to Amec Developments Limited. During the course of the development, Amec granted underleases in each of the three Blocks to the individual resident leaseholders. There were originally four parties to each of the occupational underleases, namely (1) the landlord Amec; (2) the named leaseholder; (3) the developer Countryside; and (4) the management company, SportCity. Following the sale of the last flat, Amec transferred its landlord interest to the relevant SportCity company, which then became the ground-landlord for the relevant block.

In 2013, the agents managing the blocks for the SportCity management companies asserted that there were problems with the cladding on the blocks of the apartments (remember that this was before Grenfell). Countryside did not accept that there were in fact problems but nevertheless attended the complex in March and April 2014 and undertook some works, with a further attendance in August 2017. There were three issues of legal principle in the proceedings:

1 Although they had not been named as such, SportCity claimed that the developer, Countryside Properties, were effectively a 'landlord' as the individual flat leases reserved to that company certain rights in respect of the individual flats. The occupational leases also gave Countryside an express right to impose and amend reasonable regulations regarding the use and enjoyment of properties on the estate. The leaseholders' obligations were also expressed to be made in favour of Countryside, along with the ground-landlord and management company. If Countryside could be regarded as a landlord, they would then be responsible for compliance with clause 6.1 of the lease, namely that the development will be completed and the estate laid out in accordance with plans and specifications approved by the local planning authority as well as the traditional clause 6.3 'covenant for quiet enjoyment'.
2 The claim by SportCity under the DPA was based on the alleged failings in the original construction of the buildings and whether that claim had become statute-barred, with particular relevance to the further work carried out in 2014.
3 A claim that, under the common law of tort, SportCity was entitled to damages for the cost of repairing buildings which at that point SportCity already owned but which were said to have been defectively constructed.

The total claimed by SportCity against Countryside amounted to a little in excess of £15,000,000 as the estimated cost of replacing cladding on the properties together with sums totalling approximately £840,000 in respect of cavity barrier, fire-stopping works and related items.

SportCity's claim was struck out as being time-barred. HH Judge Eyre QC saw no merit in the argument that Countryside were a landlord, even though they had not been named as such in the occupational leases. Any claim under the DPA arising out of the original construction of the estate was long time-barred as that estate had been completed in 2010 at the latest. The further work carried out in 2014 did not operate to reactivate a claim which had already been time-barred. In the Court of Appeal decision in *Alderson v Beetham Organisation Limited* [2003] Civ 408, it had previously been made clear that where further work is done, then there is a fresh cause of action in respect of that work in respect of which time runs from when the work was done but that neither the performance of that further work nor a failure to perform such work operated to revive an existing but statute-barred cause of action. The claim under the common law of tort was also found to be without merit as what is claimed was pure economic loss and as such irrecoverable in accordance with the approach laid down in *Murphy V Brentwood [1991]* 1 AC 398.

7 Fire safety and the Building Regulations 2010 (as updated)

If it is our system of town and country planning which addresses the broad question of whether a particular development should be carried out, it is the Building Regulations which deal with the minutiae of construction. The planning system is about efficient land-use and visual amenity. The Building Regulations are about ensuring that building work is carried out in a good and workmanlike manner, using appropriate materials, and that the completed building work is fit for purpose. Fire safety is barely mentioned in town planning legislation but comprises a significant part of current Building Regulations.

The modern system of building regulations began as recently as 1965 but built on a long history. For a century before modern building regulations, there were building byelaws adopted by individual local authorities but which worked to a model byelaws scheme. Like town planning, building control remains largely the preserve of local authorities, although since the 1980s, developers have had the option of appointing their own 'approved' inspector instead of using a local authority building inspector to sign off on their construction.

Modern building regulations have their statutory roots in the Building Act 1984, which superseded earlier building regulation legislation. Reference to the building regulations is now to the Building Regulations 2010, which remains the core document but has been subject to extensive tightening-up, not least in response to the Grenfell fire. Note prospective amendments contained in Part 3 of the Building Safety Act 2022 which will make extensive administrative changes, although the substance of the Building Regulations remains largely unchanged. Amongst those administrative changes are that the Health and Safety Executive will become the Building Control Authority for higher-risk buildings.

Those building regulations, as updated, comprise statements of principle merged into a mass of technical detail. The building regulations are engaged not only when there is new construction work but also where there are alterations to existing construction.

As to process, the building regulations require an initial deposit of plans and the obtaining of building regulation approval before building work starts. On satisfactory completion, a local authority building inspector will issue a completion certificate, or, in the case of an 'approved inspector', the 'final

DOI: 10.1201/9781003291893-7

certificate', evidencing the fact that the work has been satisfactorily carried out in accordance with the building regulations, at the point construction is completed.

Even though there are now many forms of household development which no longer require an express planning permission, such as small residential extensions, the building regulations apply to almost all construction work.

A useful starting point for anyone seeking to understand the building regulations is the government's *Manual to the Building Regulations*, downloadable and available at www.assets.publishing.service.gov.uk/government, which provides a code of practice for use in England. Volume 1 explains the regulatory framework.

The term 'building work' generally includes the construction of new buildings; making existing buildings bigger; altering buildings and changing what those buildings are used for. The definition also includes installing a 'controlled service' or a 'controlled fitting'. A controlled service or fitting includes a service or fitting subject to Schedule 1 to the Building Regulations in respect of sanitation, hot water safety, water efficiency, drainage and waste disposal, combustion appliances and fuel storage, conservation of fuel or power and electrical safety. A replacement window is given as an example of a controlled fitting. A boiler is given as an example of a controlled service. Renovation of thermal elements is also building work.

It is the Approved Documents published by the government which is the official source of technical guidance as to compliance with regulatory requirements, available at: www.gov.uk/government/collections/approved-documents.

As well as going through local authority building control or through the alternative of a licensed approved inspector, there are some types of work which may be done by a 'competent person', being an installer who works under a government-approved scheme. Examples of 'competent person' work include: mechanical ventilation systems; electrical work and home window replacement. Using the competent person scheme means that the person commissioning the work does not have to involve Building Control in checking the work carried out under the competent person scheme.

Anyone intending to carry out work to a building can check either with a local authority or with an approved inspector or as to whether the building regulations apply to that work. As well as building construction itself, building regulation approval may also be required for other things, such as: replacing consumer units or installing new electric circuits; installing new plumbing and waste connections; changing existing electric circuits near a bath or shower; putting in a ventilation or air-conditioning system; replacing windows and doors; replacing roof coverings on pitched and flat roofs; putting in or replacing a heating system; adding extra radiators; removing a chimney breast; removing a wall (including a wall which is non-load-bearing); creating a through lounge.

Combustion installations, such as gas boilers, must be installed to comply with the Gas Safety Installation and Use Regulations 1998 as well as the building regulations. Gas installations, such as a gas cooker, must also comply with those regulations. These regulations require that people who work on gas systems must be registered as competent, meaning that they must be on the Gas Safe Register.

Failure to comply with building regulations is a criminal offence and may also lead to other enforcement at the suit of the local authority requiring the removal or rectification of defective work.

Note that the visual quality of building work is only controlled by the building regulations to the extent that it affects technical compliance.

Whilst the legal requirements are contained in the building regulations as listed above, it is the Approved Documents which provide technical guidance for common building situations. However, that guidance may not always be appropriate where a building or an intended building is unusual in terms of its design, setting, use, scale or technology. Examples are given of the following non-standard conditions: difficult ground conditions; buildings with unusual occupancies or high levels of complexity; very large or very tall buildings; large timber buildings; some buildings that incorporate modern construction methods.

Anyone using the Approved Documents should have sufficient knowledge and skills to understand the guidance and correctly apply it to the building work, as simply following guidance does not guarantee that building work will comply with the legal requirements of the building regulations. Guidance in the Approved Documents addresses most, but not all, situations that home-owners will face. But situations may arise that are not covered in the Approved Documents.

Receiving a completion certificate or a final certificate (in the case of an approved inspector) does not guarantee compliance with building regulations. The legal meaning of the certificate is that it provides evidence, but not conclusive evidence, of compliance. The building control officer or approved inspector will not have checked every piece of building material and how it has been fitted or every aspect of the submitted documents. It is the responsibility of those carrying out building work to comply with the building regulations. The building control body will inspect the work at appropriate stages but reliance cannot be placed on this as the only method of ensuring that the work complies with the building regulations.

Home-owners in particular are advised to engage building design professionals to guide them through the complexities of construction projects. Design professionals can co-ordinate design information to reduce risks once building work has started. Anyone who designs a building should be suitably competent and skilled in order to satisfy the requirements of the building regulations.

At the point when the building work is complete, the building owner should have received a completion certificate from the local authority or a final certificate from an approved inspector. In some circumstances a building may be occupied before the building owner has received the completion certificate or final certificate. If this happens, the building owner may not be sure that the work meets all the requirements of the building regulations and this may present difficulties when re-mortgaging or selling a home. Section 76 of the Building Safety Act 2022 will require that a completion certificate must be issued before first occupation of a residential unit within a newly constructed higher-risk building, or where additional residential units have been created in such a building or where works to a building cause it to be a higher-risk building.

When existing buildings are extended or altered or the use changed, building regulations are likely to apply again. That will be the case if the work is defined as 'building work' or if the change of use comes within the scope of the building regulations. Regulation 9 of the Building Regulations exempts some small buildings, extensions and buildings for specific purposes from the Building Regulations. These exempt buildings are summarised as follows:

Class 1: buildings controlled under legislation for explosives, nuclear facilities or ancient monuments;
Class 2: certain buildings not visited by people, such as plant rooms;
Class 3: certain greenhouses, agricultural buildings and buildings for animals;
Class 4: temporary buildings not intended to remain in situ for more than 28 days;
Class 5: buildings used for site accommodation;
Class 6: certain small detached dwellings, generally without sleeping accommodation;
Class 7: certain conservatories, porches and open-sided carports.

When the building regulations apply to proposed work, the building owner needs either to involve a building control body or use an installer registered under a competent person scheme to carry out the work. It is also possible to use both a building control body and the competent person scheme on the same project.

Where unauthorised building work has been carried out after 10 November 1985, it may be possible to obtain from the local authority a Regularisation Certificate. If issued, the Regularisation Certificate will provide evidence that the works complied with the building regulations in place when the unauthorised work was carried out.

Where work is covered by the competent person scheme (such as for window replacement or re-roofing), people working under that scheme can self-certify that the work complies with building regulations. There is then no need to submit a building notice or an initial notice of deposit for plans for the work. The competent person will notify the local authority of the work and issue a completion certificate, either directly or through the scheme operator. The certificate must be given to both the building occupier and the local authority within 30 working days of completion of the work. Anyone not receiving a certificate within 30 days of completion should contact the competent person scheme operator with which that installer is registered, to help resolve the matter. Even if work is carried out under a competent person scheme, the local authority can still act if it is later found that the work contravenes building regulations.

Anyone intending to carry out building work that needs to be checked by a building control body can either deposit full plans of the proposed work or submit a Building Notice, which contains less information than full plans. Starting work without either depositing full plans or submitting a Building Notice is likely to contravene Regulation 12, which is a criminal offence. Note in particular that it is necessary to deposit full plans instead of a Building Notice if the proposed building work relates to a building to which the Fire Safety Order (FSO) applies or would apply after building work is complete.

Where full plans have been deposited, the local authority must pass or reject those plans within five weeks, or within two months if the applicant has agreed in writing to a time extension. A local authority may reject deposited plans if either the plans show that the work will contravene building regulations or the plans themselves are defective, for example, if they are incomplete or fail to show that the work will comply with the building regulations. The building work itself does not need to conform exactly to the deposit of plans but must comply with the requirements of the building regulations. If building work deviates from plans previously deposited and passed, the local authority may require that work to be taken down or altered. It is therefore advisable to consult the local authority before deviating from the approved plans.

As soon as the deposited plans have been passed, the work can begin. But there is a requirement under the building regulations to formally notify the local authority when the work has reached certain stages. The work should therefore be programmed to give the local authority time to inspect it at the required stages. If those stage notifications are not given, the local authority may require the work to be opened up for inspection to ascertain whether or not it complies with building regulations. If building work does not commence within three years of the date when the local authority passed the plans, the local authority may serve notice under Section 32 of the Building Act 1984 to rescind that approval.

Where a person carrying out building work has engaged an approved inspector licensed under the Building (Approved Inspectors) Regulations 2010, that person and the approved inspector must together give the local authority an 'initial notice', which describes the works; in the case of a new building or extension, this provides the site plan on a sufficient scale showing the boundaries and location of the site and a statement that if the work involves building over or near any drain, sewer or disposal main shown on any sewer map kept by the sewerage undertaker, that the approved inspector will consult that sewerage undertaker. After receiving an initial notice, the local authority has five working days in which to consider its validity. If the local authority does not reject the initial notice within five working days of receipt, it is presumed to have accepted the initial notice unconditionally.

Approved inspectors are prohibited from having any professional or financial interest in the workplace or its supervision and should be independent of the designer, builder or building owner, unless the work comprises any of the following: (1) the material alteration or extension of a one- or two-storey house, provided that the house has no more than three storeys when work is complete, ignoring any basement; (2) the provision, extension or material alteration of a controlled service or fitting in any building; and (3) the underpinning of a building.

If work is proposed to a building to which the FSO applies, or would apply once work is completed, the approved inspector must consult the fire authority at each of the following stages:

1   At or as soon as practicable after giving an initial notice or amended notice, together with sufficient information to show that the work will comply with Part B (Fire Safety) of the Building Regulations (see below).
2   Before giving any Plans Certificate (whether or not combined with an initial notice), the approved inspector must give the fire authority a copy of the relevant plans.
3   Before giving a Final Certificate.

Note that a 'Plans Certificate' issued by an approved inspector can be used to demonstrate that detailed plans of the work or part of it complied with the building regulations. It can provide protection if the initial notice is cancelled or ceases to be valid and no new initial notice is given or accepted. Someone proposing building work can ask an approved inspector to supply a plans certificate. If the approved inspector is satisfied with the plans, they must give a plans certificate to both the person proposing the building work and to the local authority.

When building work is complete and the approved inspector is satisfied that it meets all the relevant requirements of the building regulations, the approved inspector must give the local authority a final certificate which, like a completion certificate issued by a local authority, provides evidence but no absolute guarantee of compliance with the building regulations. The final certificate need not relate to all the work specified in an initial notice. For example, where a single initial notice covers an entire housing estate, separate final or plans certificates may be given for individual houses or groups of houses.

When it comes to fire safety, Part B of the 2010 Building Regulations, as updated, runs in tandem with the Fire Safety Order 2005. But, whereas the requirements of the FSO are on-going, it is the building regulations which provide certainty that the building construction is fire-safe as at the point when construction is completed and the building is ready for first occupation. Or, if later, the date at which any structural alterations to the building are complete. That is all the building regulations guarantee. But note that outside of the building regulations, the Building Act 1984 gives local authorities other powers in relation to unsafe buildings and structures.

Some 10 years down the line, and the construction work may no longer meet current building regulation requirements. The regulations themselves may have become more stringent to address new issues, such as those arising from the Grenfell fire. Perhaps, over time, some of that existing building work may have become defective as a result of wear-and-tear. But that is not a building regulation issue. It is an issue for a structural surveyor.

For the moment, let's go back to what the current building regulations say about fire safety. Those requirements are set out in Part B of the Building Regulations 2010, as amended to June 2022. What is set out below is the basic B1 Statement of Principles. For the expanded technical detail, go online and download the 180-page, 'Approved Document B (Fire Safety), vol. 1: Dwellings, 2019 edition including 2020 amendments', available at: www.gov.uk/ …/fire-safety-approved-document-b.

Approved Document B (Fire Safety), vol. 1: Dwellings

Let us look in detail at the bullet points in the Approved Documents.

Requirement B1: Means of Warning and Escape

The building shall be designed and constructed so that there are appropriate provisions for the early warning of fire and appropriate means of escape in case of fire from the building to a place of safety outside the building capable of being safely and effectively used at all material times.

Official advice is that regulation B1 is met by achieving all of the following:

a There are sufficient means for giving early warning of fire to people in the building.
b All people can escape to a place of safety without external assistance.
c Escape routes are suitably located, sufficient in number and of adequate capacity.
d Where necessary, escape routes are sufficiently protected from the effects of fire and smoke.
e Escape routes are adequately lit and exits are suitably signed.
f There are appropriate provisions to limit the ingress of smoke to the escape routes, or to restrict the spread of fire and remove smoke.
g For buildings containing flats, there are appropriate provisions to support a stay put evacuation strategy. The extent to which any of these measures are necessary is dependent on the use of the building, its size and its height. Building work and material changes of use subject to requirement B1 include both new and existing buildings.

Requirement B2: Internal Fire-Spread (Linings)

1   To inhibit the spread of fire within the building, the internal linings shall:

   a   Adequately resist the spread of flame over their surfaces, and
   b   Have either a rate of heat release or a rate of fire growth, which is reasonable in the circumstances.

2   Reference to 'internal linings' means the materials or products used in lining any partition, wall, ceiling or other internal structure.

Official guidance is that Regulation B2 is met by achieving a restricted spread of flame over internal linings. The building fabric should make a limited contribution to fire growth, including a low rate of heat release. It is particularly important in circulation spaces, where linings may offer the main means by which fire spreads and where rapid spread is most likely to prevent occupants from escaping. Requirement B2 does not include guidance on the following: (1) generation of smoke and fumes; (2) the upper surfaces of floors and stairs; or (3) furniture and fittings.

Requirement B3: Internal Fire-Spread (Structure)

1   The building shall be designed and constructed so that, in the event of fire, its stability will be maintained for a reasonable period.
2   A wall common to two or more buildings shall be designed and constructed so that it adequately resists the spread of fire between those buildings. For these purposes, a house in a terrace and a semi-detached house are each to be treated as a separate dwelling.
3   Where reasonably necessary to inhibit the spread of fire within the building, measures shall be taken to an extent appropriate to the size and intended use of the building, comprising either or both of the following:

   a   Subdivision of the building with fire-resistant construction;
   b   Installation of suitable automatic fire-suppression systems.

4   The building shall be designed and constructed so that the unseen spread of fire and smoke within concealed spaces in its structure and fabric is inhibited.

Official guidance suggests that Regulation B3 is met by achieving all of the following:

a   For defined periods, load-bearing elements of structure withstand the effects of fire without loss of stability.
b   Compartmentation of buildings by fire-resisting construction elements.
c   Automatic fire suppression is provided where it is necessary.

d   Protection of openings in fire-separating elements to maintain continuity of the fire separation.
e   Inhibition of the unseen spread of fire and smoke in cavities, in order to reduce the risk of structural failure and spread of fire and smoke, where they pose a threat to the safety of people in and around the building.

The extent to which any of these measures are necessary is dependent on the use of the building and, in some cases, its size, and on the location of the elements of construction.

Requirement B4: External Fire Spread

1   The external walls of the building shall adequately resist the spread of fire over the walls and from one building to another, having regard to the height, use and position of the building.
2   The roof of the building shall adequately resist the spread of fire over the roofs and from one building to another, having regard to the use and position of the building.

Official guidance is that the external envelope of a building should not contribute to undue fire spread from one part of a building to another part. This intention can be met by constructing external walls so that both of the following are satisfied:

a   The risk of ignition by an external source to the outside surface of the building and spread of fire over the outside surface is restricted.
b   The materials used to construct external walls, and attachments to them, and how they are assembled do not contribute to the rate of fire spread up the outside of the building. The extent to which this is necessary depends on the height and use of the building.

The external envelope of a building should not provide a medium for undue fire spread to adjacent buildings or be readily ignited by fires in adjacent buildings. This intention can be met by constructing external walls so that all of the following are satisfied:

a   The risk of ignition by an external source to the outside surface of the building is restricted.
b   The amount of thermal radiation that falls on a neighbouring building from window openings and other unprotected areas in the building on fire is not enough to start a fire in the other building.
c   Flame spread over the roof and/or fire penetration from external sources through the roof is restricted. The extent to which this is necessary depends on the use of the building and its position in relation to adjacent buildings and therefore the site boundary

Note: Regulation B4 is intended to be read together with the amended *Building Regulation 7 (materials and workmanship)* which now reads:

1. Building work shall be carried out

    a With adequate and proper materials which

        i Are appropriate for the circumstances in which they are used,
        ii Are adequately mixed or prepared, and
        iii Are applied, used or fixed or so as to adequately to perform the functions for which they are designed; and

    b In a workmanlike manner.
    c so that relevant metal composite material does not become part of an external wall or specified attachment, of any building.

2. Subject to paragraph 3 (below), building work shall be carried out so that materials which become part of an external wall or specified attachment of a relevant building are of European classification A2-s1d0, or A1 classified in accordance with BS EN13501–1:2007+A1:2009 (classified in accordance with the reaction to fire classification)). See below for an explanation of the British Standard classifications used in this regulation B4(2).

3. This sub-paragraph states that the special requirements contained in paragraph (2) above do not apply to: (a) cavity trays when used between two leaves of masonry; (b) any part of the roof (other than any parts of the roof which fall within paragraph (iv) of regulation 2(6) if that part is connected to an external wall); (c) door frames and doors; (d) electrical installations; (e) insulation and waterproofing materials used below ground level; (f) intumescent and fire-stopping materials where the inclusion of the materials is necessary to meet the requirements of part B of schedule 1; (g) membranes; (h) seals, gaskets, fixings, sealants and backer rods; (i) thermal break materials where the inclusion of the materials is necessary to meet the thermal bridging requirements of Part 1 of schedule 1; or (j) window frames and glass; (k) materials which form the top horizontal floor layer of a balcony which are of European Classification A1fl or A2fl-sl (classified in accordance with the reaction to fire classification) provided that the layer has an imperforate substrate under it.

In this amended building regulation B4, the term 'relevant building' is used to define a building with the storey (not including roof-top plant areas or any storey consisting of plant rooms) which is at least 18 metres above ground level and which contains any of the following:

  i One or more dwellings;
  ii An institution; or
  iii A room for residential purposes (excluding any room in a hostel, hotel or boarding house).

In this amended regulation B4, the term 'above ground level' in relation to a storey means above ground level when measured from the lowest ground level adjoining the outside the building to the top of the floor surface of the storey.

Note that the changes to Regulation B4 (which applies the more prescriptive B4(2) requirement to the materials used for buildings above a height of 18 metres) was introduced by the Building Amendment Regulations 2018 (SI 2018 No. 1230), which also re-defined the definitions of an 'external wall' of a building as well as 'specified attachment' in Building Regulation 2 (interpretation) as follows:

1 (6) In these Regulations:

    a Any reference to an external wall of a building includes a reference to

        i Anything located within any space forming part of the wall;
        ii Any decoration or other finisher applied to any external (but not internal) surface forming part of the wall;
        iii Any windows or doors in the wall; and
        iv Any part of a roof pitched at an angle of more than 70° to the horizontal if that part of the roof adjoins a space within the building to which persons have access, but not accessed only for the purpose of carrying out repairs or maintenance.

    b "specified attachment" means

        i a balcony attached to an external wall;
        ii a device for reducing heat gain within the building by deflecting heat gain within a building by deflecting sunlight which is attached to an external wall; or
        iii a solar panel attached to an external wall.

Note, BS EN 13501–1 (referred to in B4(2) above) provides the following classifications:

Class A1 products described as having no combustion to fire and which will not contribute at any stage of the fire.

Class A2 products described as having no significant contribution to fire and which will not therefore significantly contribute to the fire load and the fire growth in a fully developed fire.

Requirement B5: Access and Facilities for the Fire Service

1 The building shall be designed and constructed so as to provide reasonable facilities to assist firefighters in the protection of life.
2 Reasonable provision shall be made within the site of the building to enable fire appliances to gain access to the building.

These provisions covering access and facilities for the fire service are intended to safeguard the health and safety of people in and around the building. Their extent depends on the size and use of the building. Most firefighting is carried out within the building. Requirement B5 is met by achieving all of the following.

a   External access enabling fire appliances to be used near the building.
b   Access into and within the building for firefighting personnel to first search for and rescue people, second, to fight fire; third, provision for internal fire facilities for firefighters to complete their tasks; and, fourth, ventilation of heat and smoke from a fire in a basement.

Regulation 38(1) (Fire Safety Information) applies where building work either consists of or includes the erection or extension of a relevant building or is carried out in connection with a relevant change of use of a building and Part B of Schedule 1 imposes a requirement in relation to the work. Regulation 38(2) then requires the person carrying out the work to give fire-safety information to the responsible person no later than the date of completion of the work or (if earlier) the date of occupation of the building. Regulation 38(3) defines 'fire-safety information' as information relating to the design and construction of the building or extension, and the services, fittings and equipment provided in or in connection with the building or extension which will assist the responsible person to operate and maintain a building or extension with reasonable safety. For the purposes of Regulation 38, a 'relevant building' is a building to which the FSO applies or would apply after completion of the building work. A 'relevant change of use' is a material change of use where, after the change of use takes place, the FSO will apply or continue to apply to the building. 'Responsible person' has the meaning given by Article 3 of the FSO.

New regulatory requirements taking effect from 1 June 2022

In blocks of flats above 18 metres high, an evacuation alert system should be provided in accordance with BS8269. An evacuation alert system is a manually operated alarm system to be operated by firefighters when a fire occurs.

Blocks of flats above 11 metres high should be provided with a Secure Information Box providing firefighters with a secure facility to store information about a building. For best practice, refer to the 'Code of Practice for the Provision of Premises Information Boxes in Residential Buildings', published by the Fire Industry Association.

8 Building warranties and fire safety

Owners of new-build flats are likely to be in a better position than the owners of older flats, not only because of the statutory warranty provided by the Defective Premises Act 1972 against the party who carried out the original construction but also because of the collateral security provided by a warranty-provider such as the National House Building Council (NHBC). By new-build, we mean a flat comprised within a residential building constructed within the previous 10 years.

It is generally a mainstream mortgage-lender requirement that anyone buying a new-build dwelling, either off-plan or as a result of an onward sale has the benefit of that crucial NHBC or equivalent recognised building warranty. The initial warranty agreement will usually have been entered into between the initial contract-purchaser, the house-builder and the warranty-provider when the dwelling was still in the course of construction. The standard NHBC warranty (known as 'Buildmark') will provide the contract-purchaser with the following guarantees:

1 To underwrite the solvency of the house-builder from the date the home-buyer has agreed to acquire the property off-plan. This is important as, at contract exchange, the buyer will have paid the customary 10 per cent contract deposit to the house-builder, which will be released to the house-builder immediately to help fund the costs of construction. Without the NHBC solvency guarantee, the home-buyer would have no legal recourse against anyone if the builder became bankrupt before completion of construction and the transfer of ownership of the completed unit to the home-buyer. But note that the NHBC will only underwrite 10 per cent of the contract purchase price or £100,000 (whichever is the lower).
2 For the first two years after completion of the transaction, that the original house-builder will repair physical damage in circumstances where the construction has failed to meet the NHBC's own published performance standards. As well as putting right any construction defects, the house-builder is also under an obligation to remove any land contamination and reimburse the owner's costs in moving to temporary alternative accommodation whilst the work is carried out.

DOI: 10.1201/9781003291893-8

3 From years 3 to 10, after the initial two-year builder warranty has expired, Buildmark will continue to protect the home-buyer from damage where the property had not been built to NHBC standards. The parts of the home typically covered during this residual period are:

- Roofs
- Flues and chimneys
- Walls (including external cladding, external render and external wall-tile hanging)
- Stairs
- Ceilings (ceilings, balconies and load-bearing parts of walls)
- Glazing (double- or triple-glazing two external windows)
- Foundations
- Access (steps to the home).

If, in the 10 years following construction, the property is sold to another party, the benefit of the Buildmark warranty will pass automatically to that onward purchaser.

What Buildmark guarantees is that the property, as constructed, meets Buildmark's own stated performance standards. Crucially, those Buildmark performance standards include a warranty that the building, as constructed, meets the building regulations in force at the time of that construction, of which Part B (Fire Safety) forms part.

The additional layer of warranty protection of course only applies to those house-builders which are registered with the NHBC and automatically expires after the 10-year warranty runs out, save as regards any claims which have previously been made.

Although NHBC is currently the brand-leader for new homes warranties, covering more than 80 per cent of new homes, it is not the only lender-compliant warranty provider on the market. Other insurance-backed warranty providers are: the LABC (local authority building control) Warranty; Premier Guarantee; and Checkmate. When it comes into force, Section 144 of the Building Safety Act 2022 will require anyone carrying out a residential development to provide an insurance-backed warranty to a purchaser at the point of sale. The detail of the warranty will be set out in regulations.

The £2.2m claim brought by the leaseholders of the Fuller Court Blocks in Hornsey against the NHBC, which is currently running its course, is also a reminder that the existence of a building warranty does not always provide the peace of mind which some leaseholders expect. That particular claim arises out of alleged breaches of building regulations current at the time of construction which are claimed to represent a present or imminent danger to the physical health and safety of the occupants of Fuller Court. The issue in that case is the extent to which NHBC needed to make a suitable representative present when the opening up of the building work took place.

We have previously touched on flat-conversions and the special place which they occupy in fire-safety regulation. We now pick up on that theme because the warranty benefits provided by the NHBC and similar schemes only guarantee work carried out by registered house-builders. Whilst it is likely that many large-scale conversions will have been carried out by registered house-builders and therefore warranted, the same may not apply where an individual property-owner directly employs builders to carry out that work. That situation is now swept up by paragraphs 6.7.4 and 6.7.5 of the *UK Finance Lenders' Handbook*, which states:

6.7.4 Where the property does not have the benefit of a scheme under 6.7.1 [NHBC warranty or similar] and has been built or converted within the past 6 years, check Part 2 [individual mortgage-lender requirements] to see if we will proceed and, if so, whether you must satisfy yourself that the building work is being monitored (or where the work is completed, was monitored) by a professional consultant. If we do accept monitoring, you should ensure that the professional consultant has provided the lender's Professional Consultant's Certificate which forms an appendix to this Handbook or such other form as we may provide. The professional consultant should also confirm to you that he has appropriate experience in the design or monitoring of the construction or conversion of residential buildings and has one or more of the following qualifications:

- Fellow or Member of the Royal Institution of Chartered Surveyors (FRICS or MRICS); or
- Fellow or Member of the Institution of Structural Engineers (F.I.Struct.E or M.I.Struct.E); or
- Fellow or Member of the Chartered Institute of Building (FCIOB or MCIOB); or
- Fellow or Member of the Architecture and Surveying Institute (FASI or MASI) (only if in conjunction with a FCIOB or MCIOB qualification); or
- Fellow or Member of the Chartered Association of Building Engineers (C.Build E MCABE and C.Build E FCABE); or
- Member of the Chartered Institute of Architectural Technologists (formerly British Institute of Architectural Technologists) (MCIAT); or
- Architect registered with the Architects Registration Board (ARB). An architect must be registered with the Architects Registration Board, even if also a member of another institution, for example, the Royal Institute of British Architects (RIBA); or
- Fellow or Member of the Institution of Civil Engineers (FICE or MICE).

6.7.5 At the time he issues his certificate of practical completion, the consultant must have professional indemnity insurance in force for each claim for the greater of either:

- the value of the property once completed; or
- £250,000 if employed directly by the borrower or, in any other case, £500,000. If we require a collateral warranty from any professional adviser, this will be stated specifically in the mortgage instructions.

The Lender's Handbook also provides a pro-forma of a 'professional consultant certificate', the key warranty of which is contained in paragraph 3 of the pro-forma which states:

1 That so far as could be determined by such periodic visual inspection the property has been generally constructed:

    a   To a satisfactory standard;
    b   In general compliance with the drawings approved under the building regulations.

Finally, note the new Section 20D which the government's Building Safety Act 2022 will introduce into the Landlord and Tenant Act 1985, which will place on ground-landlords the obligation to take reasonable steps to ascertain whether money may be obtained from a third party in connection with the undertaking of remediation works, and the pursuance of that monetary claim, before passing that cost on to leaseholders.

9 Government assistance to remove defective cladding

Chancellor Rishi Sunak announced in his 27 October 2021 autumn budget the allocation of £5bn towards residential buildings with unsafe cladding, which will be part-funded by a new Residential Property Developer Tax (RPDT). which came into force on 1 April 2022. The new tax will be charged at 4 per cent on annual developer profits above £25,000,000. Provision for the new tax is contained in the Part 2 and Schedule 7 of the government's Finance Act 2022. There will be exemptions for registered social landlords.

Residential property development activities are widely defined in the Act to include, in relation to the development of new residential property: dealings in residential property; design; seeking planning permission for development; constructing or adapting residential property; marketing; managing residential property and ancillary activities. The new tax will be collected in a similar way to corporation tax and is expected to raise £2bn over a 10-year life-span.

The promised £5bn follows an earlier five-point plan, announced by Housing Secretary Robert Jenrick MP on 10 February 2021 by which the government undertook to pay for the removal of unsafe cladding for all leaseholders in high-rise residential buildings coupled with a new levy on developers and with new measures to boost the housing market. Money raised by the RPDT will be supplemented by additional income from a new levy on building control applications as provided for by Section 58 of the Building Safety Act 2022 and which will be the subject of separate government regulations.

Under these proposals (which seem to change month-by-month), the government would fully fund the cost of replacing unsafe cladding for all leaseholders in buildings over 18 metres (six storeys) in England. This is to ensure that funding is targeted at the buildings at highest risk. And there have been subsequent government announcements suggesting that funding will be extended to residential buildings below 10 metres high. The problem so far for affected leaseholders has been the lack of clarity, as the government struggles to persuade the building industry to shoulder part of the cost.

Statistics show that buildings between 18 and 30 metres high are four times as likely to suffer a fire with fatalities or serious casualties than buildings in general. Lower-rise buildings between 11 and 18 metres with a lower risk to

DOI: 10.1201/9781003291893-9

safety will gain new protection from the costs of cladding removal. It had previously been proposed that those residents would pay for cladding removal through long-term loan-interest government-backed financial arrangements which would guarantee that no leaseholder will pay more than £50 a month towards the removal of unsafe cladding. This would also provide reassurance and security to leaseholders and mortgage-lenders. However, subsequent indications are that those leaseholders will now be eligible for grants, not loans. The government will also work with the industry to reduce the need for EWS1 forms, i.e. the external wall fire review form.

Whilst, at the time of writing, details of the proposed government assistance to residential leaseholders for the replacement of defective cladding have yet to be fleshed out, it must be assumed that the technical requirements and due process will follow the full fund guidance for applications under the Building Safety Fund for the remediation of non-ACM cladding systems (England only) and the earlier Private Sector ACM Cladding Remediation Fund, both of which have now closed to new applications. Applying the earlier guidance, it is anticipated that the new scheme could be processed as follows.

- The grant funding will cover reasonable eligible costs for the removal and replacement of unsafe cladding systems on high-rise residential properties in England.
- Funding will be provided to the Responsible Entity for each qualifying residential building: being the organisation that carries the legal obligation or right to carry out the remediation works and the right to legally recover the costs from leaseholders as a service-charge. That Responsible Entity might be the building freeholder or head leaseholder or a management company, including a right-to-manage company, who has primary responsibility for the repair of the property.
- *The fund will be only for the benefit of private leaseholders who would otherwise incur the costs of remediation through their service-charges.* Where leaseholders are not liable for the cost of remedial works under the terms of their lease, but the responsible entity for the building is a leaseholder-run right-to-manage company, the building may still be eligible for funding. Applicants from the social sector will need to have demonstrated during registration that the costs of remediation are unaffordable or a threat to financial stability. Social sector or applicants intending to claim the grant associated with leaseholders in social sector buildings should refer to the relevant guidance. Those registered providers and local authorities who have registered under that scheme due to financial viability concerns will be contacted directly and cases discussed individually and taken forward on their merits. A registered provider must have notified the Regulator of Social Housing.
- All funded projects should achieve the following objectives: protect residents through increasing pace in building safety by removing and

- replacing unsafe cladding systems; improve the leaseholder communication and engagement, deliver projects on time and budget; encourage cost recovery from those responsible.
- The Ministry of Housing, Communities and Local Government (MHCLG) (now the Department of Levelling Up, Housing and Communities) is the government department leading the administration of the fund. It will work with a Greater London Authority (GLA) in London and Homes England (HE) (outside London) to administer the fund as Delivery Partners. The GLA and HE will draw on specialist expert legal and cost consultancy support to help assess individual applications.
- MHCLG will make available an expert specialist support for applicants who need additional support to plan their remediation projects. Applicants should discuss this with their respective Delivery Partner (see above) if they believe that they would benefit from this support. If a delivery partner confirms this support will be of benefit, they will forward that request to the relevant support team. There will also be an Applicant (Client) Side Support Charter that governs such assistance, which will be made available following initial contact.
- It is considered essential that buildings with unsafe cladding are remediated as quickly as possible to ensure that residents feel safe in their homes. Full applications for funding must therefore be submitted urgently. It is accordingly likely that there will be deadlines for the submission of funding applications.
- In circumstances where deadlines cannot be met, the late applications will be considered on a case-by-case basis, provided that applicants continue to provide delivery partners with realistic but ambitious project delivery timetables and continue to keep those delivery partners fully informed about any changes to those timetables. Applicants should also be aware that where it is clear that they are making insufficient progress, MHCLG will be informed so that they can be considered for an enforcement/escalation approach, which may include referral to the local enforcement agencies or public naming.
- The MHCLG will keep demand for the fund under review and publish regular updates regarding the allocation of funding against the available budget.
- Building-owners must ensure that their leaseholders are kept fully informed of the progress of their building's application at each stage of the fund process. Where residents groups have been formed to manage remediation and building safety concerns, there should be regular engagement with leaseholders and residents regarding the building's funding application.
- As a minimum, building-owners must provide updates to leaseholders and residents at the following key milestones: registration phase; project procurement; application submitted; outcome of application received; commencement or works (with an estimated completion date); works completed.

- A leaseholder feedback form will enable individual leaseholders to get in touch with the MHCLG if they have concerns about the remediation of their buildings. It is then possible that leaseholder concerns may be followed up with building-owners through their contact with the delivery partners and the Project Management Office (PMO). Individual leaseholders will also be able to access specialist advice through the Leasehold Advisory Service.
- Funding applications can only be made by the Responsible Entity (see above) for the particular building. Applicants may also appoint a representative to lead their application day-to-day, which may be a managing-agent or the project manager leading the works. But even where a representative is appointed to lead the application, the grant funding agreement must still be signed by the Responsible Entity.
- The application process itself is split into two stages: First Stage and Second Stage.
- As part of the registration phase assessment, the MHCLG will estimate the total eligible costs for each building benchmarked against industry cost data. It will use this data to check the reasonableness of costs as part of its assessment process throughout the project life cycle.
- Significant work will be needed to get an applicant to the point where they can go out to tender for a project, including scoping the project, appointing a professional team, and developing a works specification. Applications can be made for pre-tender support if an applicant needs funding to get to this stage. Pre-tender support will only be provided to applicants who have passed registration; passed through the initial due diligence; and demonstrated that the project cannot progress without this support. Pre-tender support will be limited to 10 per cent of the estimated cost of the works.
- Applicants will need to answer questions about their legal eligibility to receive funding as regards the Responsible Entity, the ownership structure of the building, and the relevant lease-provisions. Applicants will also need to answer questions about the building itself. The MHCLG will then carry out due diligence on the information provided before offering funding for pre-tender support or full financial support for the remediation works.
- If the applicant does not proceed with the works within three months of receipt of pre-tender support or if the full application turns out to be ineligible, the MHCLG reserves the right to recoup the value of this initial pre-tender funding. Where pre-tender support helps to progress a project but a full costs application is not subsequently received, the MHCLG will not seek to recoup this funding except in special circumstances set out in the short-form funding agreement.
- Applicants can only submit a full costs application once they have gone out to tender and have a preferred contractor to carry out the remediation works. At that point the applicant will be able to provide the

required cost breakdown and answer the full works and costs-related questions.
- Whether or not applicants need pre-tender support, applicants are advised to start their applications as soon as possible after being invited to apply so that the MHCLG can proceed with the necessary first stage due diligence. This will provide comfort that the applicant is, in principle, eligible for funding.
- The project costs for which funding will be available include: access directly related to the qualifying works (such as scaffolding); removal and disposal of existing cladding; replacement materials; labour and reasonable contractor on-costs; professional team fees for qualifying items; managing-agents' fees for administering qualifying expenditure; extraordinary technical requirements which incur extra costs essential to but not normally associated with removing and replacing unsafe cladding. In all cases reasonable costs must be informed by an industry standard approach to specification and procurement of works, having regard to cost benchmarks established from comparable projects. Higher-than-expected costs will be challenged and will be subject to further scrutiny and the level of grant may be reduced.
- It is likely that the scheme will not fund: works not directly related to the remediation of unsafe cladding, even where such works are planned to be taken at the same time; other necessary fire-safety works not related to unsafe cladding; operational running costs, including those associated with interim measures such as waking watches; professional team fees in respect of non-qualifying items; managing-agents' fees in administering non-eligible works; costs which would not otherwise be recovered from leaseholders through the service-charge provisions in their leases.
- Applicants must demonstrate but they have taken all reasonable steps to recover the costs of replacing unsafe cladding from those responsible through insurance claims, warranties, legal action, etc. At the application stage, the MHCLG will ask for information regarding such steps and may seek further information to satisfy itself of the position.
- Where an applicant successfully recovers damages relating to the removal and replacement of unsafe cladding, the government will require building-owners to pay to the government any amounts which are recovered and which relate to the removal and replacement of the unsafe cladding up to the amount provided through the fund. Those payments to the government may be less any unrecovered legal fees that may have been incurred when the cost recovery efforts are successful. The MHCLG will not seek to recoup amounts recovered in litigation or settlement which do not relate to the removal and replacement of unsafe cladding. Where building-owners have already recovered damages, they should deduct relevant amounts in their applications and provide an explanation as to how this has been calculated. The MHCLG does not rule out seeking an assignment of a relevant right of action where it would be appropriate to do so.

- In assessing applications, the MHCLG will consider a range of factors including: where the applicant details match publicly held records; the applicant's legal relationship with leaseholders and whether they are obliged to pay service-charges; compliance with Subsidy Control Rules (see below); confirmation of appointment of competent professionals; whether the costs are for eligible works and reasonable; a confirmed start-on-site date or signing of works contract; how the applicant will monitor progress and evaluate costs; obtaining all statutory approvals including planning permissions; a forecast start and practical completion date; what reasonable efforts the applicant has made to recover costs from any third party who may be liable.
- Funded projects will be paid in instalments. Those projects which do not require pre-tender support will be paid into instalments namely: 80 per cent at Second Stage Full Works and Costs and with the remaining 20 per cent being paid on practical completion. Where a pre-tender support has been offered, 10 per cent of those estimated costs will be paid at registration for the project, to be covered by a Short Form Fund Agreement. Two further payments covered by the Grant Funding Agreement will then be paid, namely 70 per cent for the Stage 2 Full Works Costs (when the works contract is signed) and the remaining 20 per cent at practical completion. There is also a third alternative scenario in circumstances where a chosen contractor has requested different payment schedule terms or where the applicant is otherwise unable to operate the terms set out above. The applicant should contact the delivery partner (GLA or HE) to discuss alternative payment scheduling.
- Following approval of a formal application, the applicant will receive a letter confirming approval from MHCLG, which can be used as 'in principle' proof of funding to enable signing of the works contract.
- Subsidy control is an international obligation which restricts the ways in which the UK government can subsidise UK businesses where this is likely to unfairly distort competition in particular as regards the subsidies chapter of the UK-EU Trade and Cooperation Agreement (TCA). It replaces the Europe-wide State Aid rules which previously applied during the UK's membership of the European Union, which ceased with effect from 1 January 2021, save as regards the terms of the Withdrawal Agreement. Funding provided for the benefit of leaseholders who are owner-occupiers is not affected as it is not a business subsidy. But to receive the funding, the leaseholder must be liable to meet the costs of remediation through leasehold service-charges. But funding for the benefit of buy-to-let landlords, leases of commercial premises and housing associations continue to fall within the subsidy rules, either on the basis of Small Amounts of Financial Assistance or Services of Public Economic Interest (SPEI). Accordingly, the MHCLG will require declarations from leaseholders who lease commercial premises. Leaseholders of residential premises which are let out instead of being owner-occupied will also be

required to provide declarations where they have received financial state subsidy within the previous three years including anything for cladding remediation. Applicants for grant funding must accordingly provide a list to the Delivery Partners (GLA or HE) of all leaseholders to whom they believe the subsidy rules will apply and their proportion of the total service-charge liability in the form of an Economic Actor Schedule, together with their best assessment as to whether they operate residential or commercial activities. This will include any residential leaseholder to whom the applicant believes the subsidy rules will apply who has not provided a declaration, as well as any leaseholders who have returned the signed subsidy declaration during the leaseholder consultation period that the applicant did not originally list. Beneficiaries who provide SPEIs (see above) are not subject to a cap on the amount of funding they can receive. However, where any SPEI subsidy is 15 SDR or above, then details will need to be provided on the UK's subsidy database. This shall be relevant for remediation funding where Registered Providers of Social Housing (RPs), or, exceptionally, other organisations with a charitable purpose would be liable for the costs of remedial works by virtue of their service-charge obligations. Note that SDR is an abbreviation of 'Special Drawing Rights' which is an artificial unit of currency used by the International Monetary Fund.

- If the replacement of defective cladding can be regarded as a 'snagging' item, it will be zero-rated for the purposes of VAT. Otherwise it will be standard-rated. Snagging relates to the correction of faults which are often carried out after a new building has been completed. Provided the replacement cladding forms part of the original construction and the person requesting the cladding has an interest in the building during the original construction works, then the replacement cladding may qualify for zero rating. This work may form part of the building contract with zero-rated VAT. Applicants seeking advice on whether their replacement cladding meets the criterion of snagging and is therefore eligible for zero rating can write to their HMRC Clearance Team.
- Where projects are not progressing quickly enough, the MHCLG will work with local authorities and fire and rescue services to ensure that they are considering enforcement action in relation to any unremediated unsafe high-rise building. Note that local authorities have enforcement powers under the Housing Act 2004 as extended to unsafe external wall systems by the Fire Safety Act 2021.
- There are two fund application portals, one for London, administered by the GLA and another for outside of London, administered by HE. Applicants will be given access to the relevant application portal. This access will be included in the communication to applicants who are invited to apply by the GLA or HE following completion of technical due diligence at registration.
- The Building Safety Fund process required applicants to self-certify critical aspects concerning the project and application. For example, that

the works will comply with fund requirements and also that all parties contracted to deliver remediation have complied with the requirements of their respective contracts. In order to provide this reassurance to MHCLG, applicants are advised to put in place processes that capture the evidence needed to enable them to self-certify. Those processes should also help applicants to confirm that suitable management of the works is in place and that the remediation will be completed correctly in accordance with fund requirements.

- Contractors must ensure that all non-conformances or defects are reported and demonstrate to the project manager they have been satisfactorily resolved. Applicants must ensure that their contractor implements and confirms a system for the provision of evidence at all points throughout the works, debt management and project administration arrangements. This could include a job-centric checklist, such as an inspection and test plan, that will be used to record progress of the works. Once works are complete, a certificate should be signed between the applicant and the contractor to confirm that the works had been completed to the required standard outlined in the fund requirements. The Grant Funding Agreement will require applicants to warrant that their confirmations to the self-certification statements are correct and accurate.
- Applicants are required to use competent professionals on their projects and the MHCLG will rely on the information they produce as evidence of the accuracy of information provided as part of the application. Competent professionals will also be required to sign off project works and all relevant documentation. The expression 'competent professional' refers to someone who is: qualified in their field; or a member of a professional body; who has professional Indemnity Insurance; is knowledgeable and has significant experience relevant to work-specific technical aspects; is aware of the current state of knowledge in their field; and has accumulated sufficient experience to be recognised as having a successful track record. Simply having worked in a field or having an intelligent interest in it does not by itself make someone a competent professional. Whilst due weight will be given to an opinion offered by the applicant's competent professional, for example, by signing off grant-funded works, it would not necessarily be conclusive of the issue. Further inquiry may still be needed for MHCLG and delivery partners to be fully satisfied and a material point.
- Delivery partners (GLA or HE) will require applicants to submit their applications online through their portals if they have registered their buildings and those buildings meet the technical eligibility criteria as assessed by MHCLG.
- The First Stage involves a prospective applicant being invited to submit their application. Following due-diligence checks, the MHCLG will contact the applicant as regards any missing information and provide support, if needed, to resolve any outstanding issues. That first stage could

also involve an initial legal due diligence to determine eligibility. If an applicant meets the legal eligibility criteria and has indicated that they need pre-tender support, the MHCLG will offer it at this stage up to 10 per cent of the total eligible costs for the building. Applicants will be required to provide a plan showing the footprint of the building and identifying residential properties within the building. Leasehold service-charge provisions will be checked and applicants will be required to identify four different properties which are held on residential leases representative of all the residential leases granted within the building.

- On receipt of an application for grant funding, the Delivery Partner will undertake a process of legal due diligence in which their legal adviser will review at least one of the sample leases provided to ensure that the effect of the grant will be to relieve leaseholders of a financial burden which they would otherwise face. That legal due diligence will also verify that the applicant is the correct contracting party and will review title information. At the same time the legal due diligence will review information provided in the context of Subsidy Control (see above), to ensure that in relevant cases, funding is limited to the maximum allowed grant amount of £350,000 Special Drawing Rights over three consecutive financial years (see above). Leaseholders affected by Subsidy Control will be notified of the value of the state funding they will receive.
- The applicant for the grant-funding is also required to provide details of a nominated bank account held in trust for the leaseholders into which the grant will be paid, with evidence either that this complies with the requirements of Section 42 of the Landlord and Tenant Act 1987 (service-charge contributions to be held in trust) or a client money account registered under a Client Money Protection Scheme (such as the scheme operated by the Royal Institution of Chartered Surveyors which provides protection as a last resort where an RICS-regulated firm is unable to repay a client's money). Note that it is the Housing and Planning Act 2016 and the Client Money Protection Schemes for Property Agents (Approval and Designation of Schemes) Regulations 2018 which govern the making of such schemes.
- For the Second Stage of the application process, applicants must provide a firm proposal, including a detailed costed-out project plan. Again there is an initial on-line self-certification process. It is at this stage that the applicant is also required to provide the subsidy control information. This must also include confirmation that a 'competent professional' has certified that the planned remediation design and works comply with relevant technical requirements for a replacement cladding system and that the applicant has formal written evidence of this which is available on request.
- Information applicants must keep on file include: the Specification or Employer's Requirements; evidence of written sign-off of the specification or employer's requirements by a competent professional; information on the fire-safety classification of the replacement cladding material; information

on the fire-safety classification of the replacement or any retained installation; information on the fire-safety classification of the replacement or retained sheathing board. Applicants must also maintain a Project Directory of existing and proposed professional team appointments and confirm that such directory is available on request.
- The MHCLG must be advised if the works require planning approval. If so, that planning approval must be in place before works start on site. Alternatively there must be formal written confirmation that the proposed works do not require planning approval.
- The applicant must confirm that the fund's standard contract requirements have been included within the Works Contract with the main contractor. That works contracts must also be kept on file. Applicants must also confirm and explain their procurement strategy, such as whether the procurement is 'traditional' (where contractors tender for carrying out of works on the basis of a pre-designed specification); 'design and build' (where contractors tender against partially completed design information on the basis that the appointed contractor will take responsibility for completing that design and carrying out the works); or whether an alternative procurement option has been adopted. However a contractor is appointed, that contractor must have the required professional Indemnity Insurance. Applicants must also explain their tender strategy (whether by obtaining quotes or an open tender process or by an alternative process of negotiation or other third way).
- The complete full works and costs spreadsheet provided by MHCLG must be uploaded to calculate the project costs and with an appropriate contingency sum which must also be included. There must also be confirmation from a 'competent professional' that the contract sum represents a reasonable sum for the cost of the works, given the current market conditions, taking into account the qualifications or exclusions and the evidence of this is available on request.
- Once the MHCLG has made a decision on a grant application, they will write setting out their decision and next steps. If the application is successful, the applicant will then be required to complete and sign a Grant Funding Agreement including ancillary documents (such as standard form collateral warranties and a Duty of Care Deed from the costs consultant). A request for a drawdown of approved funds may be made once the grant funding agreement is completed and all relevant conditions have been met.
- Following the award of funding and the signing of the grant funding agreement, the MHCLG will require the applicant to enter into a works contract in the form required.
- Once the project is underway, applicants must provide project management information on a regular basis, which will be used to monitor progress and costs. The MHCLG will use that data to understand where projects are not proceeding to plan and triage support to those projects

which might need it. That support could include Applicant (Client) Side Support to help progress projects.
- Applicants are required to manage project costs within the amount of the grant awarded. If there are unforeseen costs overruns or variations to contract scope, applicants may submit an application for variation to maximum grant sums to the delivery partner. The MHCLG will then confirm in writing if these variations are approved. Variations may be approved: to comply with statutory requirements or to replace qualifying unsafe cladding from areas not previously identified. Variations arising from other reasons are unlikely to qualify for additional funding.
- At practical completion of the project, applicants must provide evidence of sign-off from a competent professional and from building control. After completion, a sample of projects may be randomly selected or targeted for potential government audit, the funding of which is not an eligible cost.

10 Buying a flat in a high-rise block

The key principle of UK property law is 'caveat emptor'. It means 'buyer beware'. Buy a car from a dealer-showroom and you are protected by a raft of sale-of-goods legislation which has evolved over a century. You will have the benefit of implied warranties that the dealer had the right to sell the car to you; that it was in the state and condition on which it was expressed to be sold; and that if it is not as advertised, you will have the right to return to the showroom to seek an immediate refund. If you buy that car using the dealer-arranged finance, you will have the protections offered by the Consumer Credit Act, which will normally include the statutory 14-day cooling-off period. Even if you have purchased the car privately, you will still have some limited statutory protections. But when you purchase your flat, the only protection you will have is what is contained in your contract of sale.

With the exception of new-build, most UK properties are sold 'as seen'. The only documents which a residential seller is required to hand over to a prospective purchaser is the energy performance certificate (EPC), which provides an official statement of the flat's energy efficiency. It is then the responsibility of a prospective buyer's conveyancer to carry out a detailed investigation of the seller's title to ensure that it is 'good and marketable' and that there will be no unpleasant surprises for the buyer after they have completed the transaction and moved into the property. 'Good and marketable' means that the title to the property would be mortgageable and therefore saleable. The two generally go hand-in-hand. A defective property title which would not meet mainstream mortgage-lender requirements is unlikely to be saleable, except perhaps at a significant discount.

The process of title investigation will routinely include: anti-money laundering due diligence; checking the registered title of the property (assuming that the title is registered) and all associated title documentation; putting in a raft of conveyancing searches to identify anything affecting the property which may not be shown on the registered title; raising extensive pre-contract inquiries of the seller's solicitor to sweep up any other issues which may not be readily apparent, either from the registered title or the searches; and, finally, to agree the terms of the sale-contract. If anything is missed, it is the buyer's lawyer who is likely to face a professional negligence claim. It is why

DOI: 10.1201/9781003291893-10

conveyancing insurance is so prohibitively expensive. If something adverse is picked up from those routine conveyancing enquiries, the buyer's conveyancer will need to explain the issue to the buyer (and mortgage-lender) to ensure that they are fully aware and take further express instructions as to whether that client still wishes to proceed.

What Grenfell has done is to impose an extra layer of due diligence on the pre-contract inquiries which a buyer's lawyer is required to carry out before contracts can safely be exchanged on the purchase of a flat in a multi-occupied building. Before Grenfell, buyers' conveyancers would have had no reason to suspect that defective external wall insulation was even an issue. But that has all changed since Grenfell. When it comes to fire safety, the buyer's lawyer's additional conveyancing responsibilities now cover the following:

1   To pick up any actual fire-safety risks within the building. This might include enquiries as to who is legally responsible for fire safety within the building and to obtain and review copies of any fire-risk assessments. When it is brought into force, Section 78 of the Building Safety Act 2022 and its associated regulations will establish a public register of higher-risk buildings.
2   To identify any actual or foreseeable service-charge liabilities arising out of expected capital expenditure in putting right an identified fire-risk, the cost of which will be shared between individual leaseholders.
3   To ensure that there is no identified fire-risk which, whilst it remains unresolved, would prevent the property being accepted by a mainstream mortgage-lender.

For most residential transactions, pro-forma pre-contract conveyancing enquiries are set out in the Law Society-recommended TA6 (Property Information Form), as supplemented by the TA7, which asks additional questions for residential leasehold properties. In both the TA6 and TA7, the notable omissions are any detailed questions about fire safety. The forms are intended to be 'all-purpose', with questions framed in general rather than specific terms.

For commercial property transactions, including possibly the investment purchase of a block of flats, conveyancers are more likely to use the Commercial Standard Property Enquiries (CPSEs) formulated by the British Property Federation. Fire safety features in Section 11 of CPSE1, which applies to all property transactions, but only in the briefest of terms. Section 11 of CPSE1 states:

> 11.1
> Please advise us where we may inspect any records in relation to the Property, made for the purposes of complying with the Fire Safety Order 2005, including any records of findings following a fire risk assessment of the Property.

11.2
Please advise us where we may inspect any records in relation to any premises within any building of which the Property comprises part, made for the purposes of complying with the Fire Safety Order 2005, including any records of findings following a fire risk assessment of any such premises.

11.3
Please provide details of any steps taken in relation to the Property to co-operate with any other people and to co-ordinate measures to comply with the Fire Safety Order 2005.

11.4
What are the current means of escape from the Property in case of emergency?

11.5
If any current means of emergency escape from the Property passes over any land other than the Property or a public highway please:

a   provide copies of any agreements that authorise such use;
b   confirm that all conditions in any such agreements have been complied with; and
c   provide details of anything that has occurred that may lead to any agreement for means of escape being revoked, terminated or not renewed.

Reference to fire safety also receives brief mention in the Law Society's updated Leasehold Property Enquiries Form LPE1. Tucked away in the section on buildings insurance are the following questions:

5.6.1

i   Has a fire-risk assessment been completed?
ii Has an external wall fire risk assessment been completed?

5.6.2

i   If yes, have urgent or essential works been recommended?
ii Have these been completed?

The seller's answers to the questions given on the LPE1 are then summarised in a statement of financial matters given to the leasehold-purchaser using the Law Society-recommended one-page LPE2.

It follows that a conveyancer acting on the purchase of a residential flat comprised within a high-rise building must give careful consideration to the fire-risk implications and consider what additional questions are appropriate to ensure that they are able to report back fully to the buyer and mortgage-lender on those issues before contracts are exchanged.

A starting point is the *UK FINANCE Mortgage Lenders' Handbook for Conveyancers*, which is continually updated and available for free download at: www.lendershandbook.ukfinance.org.uk/lenders-handbook. Part 1 of the handbook contains standard requirements applicable to all mortgage-lenders. Part 2 of the handbook provides the specific additional requirements of named mortgage-lenders. Part 3 of the handbook deals with the rarer situation where a conveyancer is acting only for a mortgage-lender, and not jointly for the buyer and mortgage-lender. When it comes to fire safety, mortgage-lenders' requirements are summarised in the following single paragraph:

> The external wall fire review process requires a fire safety assessment to be concluded by a suitably qualified and competent professional and confirmed using the EWS [external wall system] Form. It delivers assurance for lenders, valuers, residents, buyers and sellers. The form has been developed through extensive consultation with a wide range of stakeholders, including fire engineers, lenders and valuers and other cross-industry representatives. Only one assessment will be needed for each building and this will be valid for five years.

It follows that a satisfactory EWS1 form (see Chapter 11) has now become an essential conveyancing requirement whenever a flat is being purchased in any multi-occupied residential building. Arguably, the only exception might be completion of a flat purchase from a mainstream registered house-builder which has been constructed in accordance with the most up-to-date building regulations and which is guaranteed by a 10-year building-warranty.

11 The EWS1 form

The EWS1 (external wall fire review) form is approved by the Building Societies Association, the Royal Institution of Chartered Surveyors and UK FINANCE and is frequently updated. For the purposes of this book, we are working with version 2, published 8 March 2021. Its stated purpose is a set way for a building-owner to confirm to valuers and lenders that an external wall system or attachments, such as a balcony, has been assessed by a suitable expert. It is for the external wall system only. It is not a life-safety certificate. It should not be taken as confirmation that other works relating to fire safety in other parts of the building are not required. Independent advice on the fire-risk assessment of the entire building should always be obtained.

Where the expert who signs off the EWS1 form has been asked to provide the client with a separate report, the EWS1 form reflects the conclusion set out in that report. Note in particular the following disclaimer contained within the EWS1 form, which effectively means that it is only the building-owner which can place reliance on the EWS1 form, not individual flat-owners. The disclaimer reads:

> No responsibility is accepted to any third party for the whole or any part of the contents of this form. For the avoidance of doubt, the term 'third party' includes (but is not limited to) any lender who may see the form during the process through which they come to make a loan secured on any part of the Subject Address [being the name of a block of flats]; and any prospective purchaser or borrower who becomes aware of the form during the process through which they come to purchase or secure a loan against an interest in any part of the subject address. Should any third party (e.g. a buyer, seller, lender, valuer) wish to rely on this form, they should contact the signatory's organisation.

What this disclaimer effectively means is that, to derive the full protection of the EWS1, any prospective purchaser or mortgage-lender of an individual flat would need to purchase from that signatory a 'Letter of Reliance' extending the guarantees given by the EWS1 to the prospective purchaser, their successors in title, and anyone lending money on the strength of the EWS1 form.

DOI: 10.1201/9781003291893-11

The EWS1 form then contains a written warranty by the signatory that they confirm that they have used reasonable skill and care to investigate the primary external wall materials (typically insulation, filler materials and cladding) and attachments (including balconies) of the external walls of the building or block.

Following completion of the assessor's investigation, the assessor then completes either Option A or Option B of the EWS1. Option A will be completed when the assessor has concluded that the external wall materials are unlikely to support combustion. Assessors then certify that, to the best of their knowledge, the primary materials used meet the criteria of limited combustibility (as defined in BS 9991:2015) or better, and cavity barriers are installed to an appropriate standard in relevant locations. Cavity barrier fire performance and locations are to be based on relevant fire-safety design guidance documentation, such as BS 9991, or relevant statutory guidance. In relation to attachments, the assessor must certify either that there are no attachments whose construction includes significant quantities of combustible materials or that there is an appropriate risk assessment of the attachments confirming that no remedial works are required. Where, in relation to attachments, neither of the above options apply, there may be potential costs of remedial works to those attachments. In the latter scenario, the assessor should notify the client that the fire-risk assessment of the building will need to be reviewed to consider the findings of the external wall survey.

To complete Option A, an assessor must certify that they have the expertise needed to identify the relevant materials within the external wall and attachments and whether the fire-resisting cavity barriers have been installed correctly. However, this does not necessitate the need for expertise in fire engineering.

The assessor will complete Option B when it is found that combustible materials are present in the external wall. The assessor must then certify either that the identified fire-risk is sufficiently low that no remedial works are required or that the fire-risk is sufficiently high that remedial works are required and that the assessor has identified to the client the remedial and interim measures that are required, which are to be documented separately. Even where no remedial works are considered necessary, the assessor should still notify the client that the fire-risk assessment of the building will need to be reviewed to consider the findings of the external wall survey. To certify the EWS1 under Option B, an assessor requires a higher level of expertise in the assessment of fire-risk presented by external wall materials. For the Institution of Fire Engineers (IFE), this should be a Chartered or Incorporated Engineer with full membership of that institution. For non-IFE members, the assessor should be a fully qualified member of a relevant professional body that deals with fire safety in the built environment, with status either actual or equivalent to the Chartered or Incorporated Engineer status.

An assessment of fire-risk must also include, so far as is necessary, the need to ensure a reasonable standard of health and safety to those in and around the building as regards resisting and inhibiting the spread of fire within the building; to prevent the unseen spread of fire and smoke within concealed spaces; and adequately resist the spread of fire over the walls, having regard to the height, use and position of the building. The assessment must also take account of regulations and published design guidance as current at the time of construction as well as those which are current at the time of the assessment, and the EWS1 cannot guarantee that it would address guidance and regulations which may be introduced after its issue. An assessor may also consider it appropriate to provide the client with a separate report on their investigation to support statements provided in the EWS1 form. However, that separate report would not normally need to be supplied to the valuer along with the EWS1 form unless there are specific issues which require such disclosure. An EWS1 form will need to be reassessed if any significant changes occur to the external wall or attachment of the building and is otherwise valid for up to five years from the date on which it is signed.

Obtaining and reviewing an EWS1 form

One of the problems is the policy vagueness and ambiguity as to when an EWS1 form is – or is not – required. When it was first introduced in December 2019, the intention was that it would only be required for multi-let residential buildings of more than 18 metres (around six storeys) in height. If the cladding was then deemed safe, the mortgage could proceed. If not, the cladding would need to be replaced. However, later official advice suggested that the EWS1 form might also be appropriate for some multi-occupied premises of less than 18 metres in height and which do not have external cladding. To help clear up the issue, the RICS issued guidance designed to clarify which residential buildings require additional fire-safety inspections.

This guidance, which took effect from 5 April 2021, was issued in response to increasing concerns that lenders were refusing to lend unless provided with an EWS1 form, which had trapped leaseholders, who were unable to sell or re-mortgage their properties until an investigation has been undertaken and/or identified remedial works have been carried out. Accordingly. this 5 April 2021 guidance set out the RICS view as to which buildings should require an EWS1 form. Under the RICS guidance an EWS1 form is required:

- For buildings over 18 metres, unless the building was signed off under the Building (Amendment) Regulations 2018.
- Buildings over six storeys with either cladding or curtain wall glazing or vertically stacked balconies made from or connected by combustible materials, such as timber.
- Buildings of five or six storeys with either a significant amount of cladding (being approximately one-quarter of the entire elevation) or panels made from aluminium composite material; metal composite material; high-pressure laminate or vertically stacked balconies made from or connected by combustible materials.

- Buildings of four storeys or fewer with panels made from ACM, MCM or HPL. Where metal cladding is present, written confirmation should be obtained from the building-owner or manager that panels made from those materials have not been used.

One of the reasons why an EWS1 form is both slow and expensive to obtain is that it involves an invasive process which has to be commissioned by the party responsible for the building, not an individual flat-owner. The guidance notes for the completion of an EWS1 form state that investigation must include evidence of the fire performance of the actual materials installed. For both Options A and B, this will often include either a physical inspection by the signatory to the EWS1 form or inspection of photographic or similar information gathered by a third party, provided that the assessor can have sufficient confidence in that third party. This will also include the standards of construction of key fire-safety installations, such as cavity barriers. Given the nature of external walls, this would typically involve investigations into a limited number of locations to be determined by the assessor. Review of designs may assist but on their own would not be sufficient. If the wall construction includes multiple wall types, the investigation should include each type.

As a flat-owner cannot apply for an EW1S form directly, obtaining such certification is dependent on the willingness of the building-owner to commission that formal assessment on behalf of all the leaseholders in the block. This might not be a problem if the block is managed collectively by the leaseholders through a management company but might be problematic if the ground-landlord is a remote third party. Then there is the cost of the commissioning of the EWS1 form, which will be substantial because of the amount of work involved. Unless this initial cost is met by the flat-owner requesting the EWS1 survey, that cost will need to be shared by all of the leaseholders through the annual service-charge. If the cost to each individual leaseholder is more than £250, that cost may need to be the subject of a formal Section 20 consultation under the Landlord and Tenant Act 1985.

Even where there is agreement between leaseholders on the need to commission the carrying-out of an EWS1 assessment, there may be other practical difficulties in getting that assessment done quickly. A significant issue is the scarcity in the number of qualified fire-safety inspectors able to carry out this work and the millions of flats which are affected. The certificates themselves can cost upwards of £10,000 and there are examples of building-managers being asked to wait for up to 10 years for one to become available.

There is also the extreme diligence required on the part of a buyer's conveyancer to scrutinise the information contained within an EWS1 form, even when it does exist, and to know what advice to give to a buyer or a prospective mortgage-lender to enable them to make an informed decision before contracts are exchanged. The mere existence of an EWS1 form is not enough. It is the information contained within it which is crucial.

Although an EWS1 form is stated to last for five years, that itself might not provide sufficient comfort to a mortgage-lender if, at the point contracts are exchanged, the EWS1 form has only one or two years left to run. So under current official guidance, the cost of obtaining of successive EWS1 forms is likely to be a recurring and unwanted liability for every residential leaseholder in a high-rise block.

12 Private landlord responsibilities relating to fire safety

When we refer to residential letting, we are generally referring to residential tenancies of less than seven years which are predominantly regulated by the assured shorthold regime introduced by the Housing Act 1988 (which has survived several changes of government) and (where applicable) by the Housing Act 2004, which governs lettings involving houses in multiple occupation (HMOs). The two statutory regimes overlap. An assured shorthold tenancy (or AST), which can be terminated on as little as two month's notice, can be granted to an occupant of an HMO as it can to any other residential property.

It is also a sector which, over the past 30 years, has become increasingly regulated, with many traps for the amateur landlord and severe financial consequences for non-compliance. That regulation now covers tenancy deposits; energy-efficiency; information as to tenants' rights and, of course, fire safety. To make things that little bit more difficult, modern residential tenant legislation is not stored in a single place but spread across a wide range of statutes and regulation. In this chapter we attempt to pull those threads together so far as they relate to fire safety. Anyone intending to rent an apartment in a multi-occupied residential building will now routinely be provided with the following documents in addition to the tenancy agreement itself:

- the Energy Performance Certificate (or EPC) (which grades the energy-efficiency of the unit into one of several of bands);
- Electrical Safety Certificates (see below);
- Gas Safety Certificates (see below);
- tenancy deposit scheme;
- 'How to Rent' booklet explaining in plain language a tenant's rights and responsibilities;
- fire-safety information relating to the building.

The general rule for short-term lettings is that statutory responsibility for fire safety will always rest with the residential landlord. Nor is it likely that a short-term residential tenant will ever face the crippling service-charges which

DOI: 10.1201/9781003291893-12

108 *Private landlord responsibilities*

millions of UK leaseholders face for replacement of defective cladding and other capital-intensive fire-safety measures. This is partly because of Section 11(1) of the Landlord and Tenant Act 1985 which places the following statutory maintenance and repair responsibilities on a residential landlord:

> 11(1) In a lease [tenancy] to which this section applies [being for a term not exceeding seven years] there is implied a covenant by the Lessor [landlord]:
>
> a   To keep in repair the structure and exterior of the dwelling house (including drains, gutters and external pipes);
> b   To keep in repair and proper working order the installations in the dwelling house for the supply of water, gas, and electricity and for sanitation (including basins, sinks, baths and sanitary conveniences, but not other fixtures, fittings and appliances for making use of the supply of water, gas or electricity);
> c   To keep in repair and proper working order the installations in the dwelling house for space heating and heating water.

If it is Section 11 which places legal responsibility on the residential landlord (at least as regards the structure and exterior of the building), the extent of that legal responsibility is dependent on the physical type of the premises which are being let and how those premises are being occupied. Those responsibilities will arise under the Fire Safety Order (FSO) (where applicable); as supplemented by the Housing Act 2004 (where the premises comprise an HMO) and the electricity and gas safety regulations which are explained later in this chapter.

Note the specific exemption from the FSO of 'domestic premises', which are defined as premises 'occupied as a private dwelling (including any garden, yard, garage, outhouse or other appurtenance to such premises which is not used in common by the occupants of more than one such dwelling)'.

So there would be complete exemption from the FSO to a letting of a house to a single household. However, that exemption is not absolute in relation to premises comprising either a flat or a house in multiple occupation because of Article 31 (10) of the FSO, which disapplies that exemption to the ability of an enforcing authority to serve notice prohibiting occupation when of the opinion that the use of the premises involves or will involve a risk to occupants so serious that the use of the premises ought to be prohibited or restricted. Nor in such circumstances does the general exemption prevent the ability of an inspector to enter premises under Article 27 of the FSO.

Additional fire-safety responsibilities apply to houses in multiple occupation (HMOs), which are defined as property rented out by at least three people who are not from the same household (e.g. a family) who share facilities like the bathroom or kitchen. In England and Wales, a residential landlord must have a licence under the Housing Act 2004 to rent out a 'large HMO'. An HMO is classed as 'large' if all of the following criteria apply:

i   the premises are rented out to five or more people who are from more than one household;
ii   Some or all of the tenants shared bathroom or kitchen facilities;
iii   At least one tenant pays rent (or an employer pays rent on their behalf).

'Large' HMOs must be licensed by the local authority and it will always be a condition of such licence that:

- The landlord must provide an updated gas-safety certificate for each year.
- The landlord must install and maintain smoke alarms.
- The landlord must provide safety certificates for all electrical appliances when requested.

Gas Safety Certificates

A residential landlord's responsibility for gas safety within tenanted property is set out in detail in Regulation 36 of the Gas Safety (Installation and Use) Regulations 1998, as amended. Those duties are summarised in the HSE's (Health and Safety Executive) April 2018 publication 'A Guide to Landlord's Duties: Gas Safety (Installation and Use) Regulations 1998 as amended Approved Code of Practice and Guidance'.

The duties generally apply to appliances and flues provided for tenants' use in 'relevant premises', essentially meaning any lease not exceeding seven years' duration. A landlord's regulatory responsibilities are then to do the following:

- Ensure gas fittings and flues are maintained in a safe condition. Gas appliances should be serviced in accordance with the manufacturer's instructions. If such instructions are not available, it is recommended they are serviced annually unless otherwise advised by a Gas Safe-registered engineer.
- Ensure that an annual safety check is carried out on each gas appliance and flue. Before any new tenancy starts, to make sure that these checks have been carried out within one year before the start of the tenancy date, unless those appliances have been installed for less than 12 months, in which case they should be checked within 12 months of the installation date.
- Keep the record of the gas-safety check until two further checks have been carried out (which may be longer than two years).
- Issue a copy of the latest Gas Safety Check Record within 28 days of the check being completed, or to any new tenant before they move in (in some cases with there being an option to display the record).

The 2018 Amendment Regulations enable landlords to have the annual gas-safety check carried out any time from 10–12 calendar months after the previous check and still retain the original deadline date as if the check had been carried out exactly 12 months after the previous check.

The safety check and maintenance requirements generally apply to any gas appliance or flue installed in the relevant premises, save items owned by the tenant. However, the safety check requirement does not apply to appliances (such as communal heating) which serve relevant premises but are situated off-site. Such statutory safety responsibility cannot be contracted back to a residential tenant. Landlords are also urged to ensure that tenancy agreements allow them access to relevant premises to enable maintenance or safety checks to be carried out.

Landlords are under a duty to take 'all reasonable steps' to ensure that essential safety checks and maintenance are carried out, which may involve giving written notice to a tenant requesting access and explaining the reason. Landlords are advised to keep a record of any action in case the tenant refuses access and a landlord has to demonstrate what steps have been taken. If a tenant continues to refuse access after repeated contact, the landlord may need to consider court action through the terms of the individual tenancy agreement as the regulations themselves give landlords no power to force entry to premises.

The engineer carrying out the check must be Gas Safe-registered. The safety-check record will contain details of any defects which are identified and remedial action taken. Landlords are recommended to retain copies of work done to rectify defects identified by a safety check. It is a criminal offence for a landlord to use, or allow the use of, a gas appliance known to be unsafe. Under no circumstances should a landlord connect an appliance identified as unsafe, which has either been isolated or disconnected for safety reasons, until the fault has been rectified.

Electrical Safety Certificates

Legislation placing responsibility on a residential landlord for the safety of electrical-installations within a let-property were introduced by the Electrical Safety Standards in the Private Rented Sector (England) Regulations 2020, which took effect 1 June 2020.

Regulation 3 places responsibility on a private landlord who grants or intends to grant a residential tenancy to ensure that electrical safety standards are met for the duration of the tenancy and that every electrical installation is inspected and tested at intervals no more than five years apart. The first inspection must take place before the first letting of the premises and the landlord must provide a formal report of every inspection to each existing as well as each prospective tenant before they move into the property. Where the report highlights a danger in relation to any electrical installation, the landlord must ensure that the necessary remedial work is carried out within 28 days, or sooner if recommended in the report. The regulations also give the local housing authority certain default powers to act in cases where a landlord is in default.

The Furniture and Furnishings (Fire) (Safety) Regulations 1988

These regulations impose requirements in relation to new domestic furniture. In summary:

- No furniture (other than mattresses, bed-bases, pillows and cushions) may include upholstery which does not pass the 'cigarette test' as defined in the regulations.
- No furniture other than pillows and cushions may include any filling material which fails the relevant ignitability tests as defined in the regulations and no furniture may include, as filling, any crumb foam which is not derived from combustion-modified foam.
- Loose filling material may not be supplied for filling pillows or cushions or upholstering or re-upholstering furniture if it fails the relevant ignitability test or if it contains crumb foam not derived from custom-modified foam.
- If furniture (other than mattresses, bed-bases, pillows and cushions) is supplied with a permanent cover, the cover must pass the match test as defined unless the cover is made of a specified material and the furniture has an interliner which passes the regulatory test.
- No cover of fabric intended to replace the permanent cover on furniture may be supplied unless the cover or a fabric passes the match test or the furniture has an interliner which passes the regulatory test and is of a specified material.
- Covers other than permanent covers for furniture, except mattresses, bed-bases, pillows and cushions, must pass the appropriate match test.
- The appropriate regulatory display label is to be attached to furniture other than mattresses, bed-bases, pillows and cushions which is being sold by retail.
- Permanent labels are to be attached to furniture (except mattresses and bed-bases) and upholstery and to covers (other than permanent covers) and if the label is not in the longer regulatory form, the additional information must be supplied to an enforcement authority if required.
- Manufacturers and importers must supply regulatory information to an enforcement authority if required to do so.
- Second-hand furniture must also comply with regulatory requirements.

The Smoke and Carbon Monoxide Alarms (England) Regulations 2015

These regulations impose a requirement on residential landlords to ensure that a smoke alarm is equipped on every storey of the building and a carbon monoxide alarm is equipped in any room which contains a solid fuel-burning combustion appliance. The landlord also has to ensure that these alarms are in proper working order at the start of a new tenancy.

Fitness for Human Habitation and Category Fire Hazards

The Homes (Fitness for Human Habitation) Act 2018 introduced a new Section 9A into the Landlord and Tenant Act 1985 imposing on residential landlords a new implied warranty in every tenancy agreement that the dwelling is fit for human habitation at the time the tenancy is granted and that it will remain so during the term of the tenancy. What actually makes a dwelling 'fit for human habitation' is defined in Section 10 of the 1985 Act which, as recently extended, now includes: repair; stability; freedom from damp; internal arrangements; natural lighting; ventilation; water supply; drainage and sanitary conveniences; facilities for preparation and cooking of food and for disposal of waste; and the absence of any 'Prescribed Hazard'.

Any significant fire-risk falls within the definition of 'Prescribed Hazard', as currently defined by the Housing Health and Safety Rating System (England) Regulations 2005, which lists 29 categories of hazard. Those identified hazards presenting the most imminent and serious danger are classed as Category 1 Hazards. The less serious or less-imminent hazards are classed as Category 2 Hazards.

The specified 29 classes of residential hazard are listed in Schedule 1 of the Rating Regulations. Of most relevant to fire safety are:

- Class 24: exposure to or uncontrolled fire and associated smoke.
- Class 25: contact with controlled fires or flames; hot objects; liquid or vapours.
- An explosion at the dwelling or HMO.

Index

agencies 42, 89
agricultural buildings 74
air tightness 3
Airbnb 54
air-conditioning systems 72
aircraft 17
alarm systems 3, 23, 38, 82, 109, 111
Alderson v Beetham Organisation Ltd 70
alert systems 2, 38, 82
alterations: notices (art 29 FSO) 30–1; restrictions on 53
aluminium composite material (ACM) 3, 9, 104
Amec Developments Ltd 69
amenity areas 51–2, 55, 71
ancient monuments 74
animals 74
appeals 32; (arts 35–36 FSO) 34
Applicant (Client) Side Support Charter 89
application portals 93–4
appraisals, fire-risk 40, 42–4, 47
architects 42, 85
Architects Registration Board (ARB) 85
architectural technologists 42, 85
arrears 55–6, 61
assured shorthold tenancy (AST) 107
audio-equipment 54
audit: government 97

backer rods 80
balconies 4, 17, 41, 52, 55, 80–1, 84, 102–4
Ballymore 2
bankruptcy 1, 83
basements 4, 76, 82
basins 108
bathrooms 108–9
baths 72, 108
battens 4–5
bed-bases 111

behavioural issues 54
bills 1, 49, 56–7
bin-stores 52
blankets 12
boarding houses 80
boiler rooms 17–18
boilers 18, 72
breach of duty/obligations 35, 50, 55–6, 62–3, 67
brick 43
British Institute of Architectural Technologists 85
British Property Federation 99
British Standards Institute (BSI) 42–3, 80
buckets, fire 12
budgets 59, 87, 89
building regulations 71–82; access and facilities for fire service 81–2; approved documents 77–82; exempt buildings, classes of 74; external fire spread 79–81; internal fire-spread (linings) 78; internal fire-spread (structure) 78–9; means of warning and escape 77; new regulatory requirements (from 2022) 82; stages 76
Building Safety Act (2022) 65–6
Building Safety Charge 65–6
building warranties 83–6; guarantees 83; parts of the home covered 84; UK Finance Lenders' Handbook 85–6
building work: definition 72, 74
Buildmark 83–4
buy-to-let landlords 6–7, 92
byelaws 71; suspension of (art 44 FSO) 36
buying a flat in a high-rise block 98–101; conveyancing responsibilities 99

cables 3
capital: expenditure 58, 99; works 56, 66

carbon monoxide alarms 111
caretakers 15, 17–18
carports 74
Category Fire Hazards 112
caveat emptor 98
cavities 79; barriers 4–5, 70, 103, 105; trays 80
ceilings 52, 78, 84
cement 4
certificates *see* electrical safety certificates; gas safety certificates; life-safety certificate
chartered surveyors 59, 85, 95, 102–3
chemical substances 23
children 5
chimneys 72, 84
cigarette test 111
civil liability 35, 67; for breach of statutory duty (art 39 FSO) 35
cladding 1–4, 6–10, 12–3, 23, 40, 42–5, 47, 56–8, 67–9, 84, 87–97, 103–5, 108
combustibility 4, 45, 103
combustible material 10, 45, 47, 103–4
combustion 72, 81, 103, 111; appliances 72, 111; installations 72; modified foam 111
commercial: activities 93; agreements 61; buildings 41; lettings 65; premises 65, 92; property 99; space 2; standard 99
Commercial Standard Property Enquiries (CPSEs) 99
Commonhold and Leasehold Reform Act 63
common-law rights 56
communal: areas 39, 49–50, 54; drainage 52; facilities 52; heating 52, 110; parts of buildings 14, 17–18, 38, 55, 62, 64, 68
compartmentation 10, 13, 78
competence 14, 26, 44–5; competent persons 14–6, 20, 23–4, 26, 41, 43–5, 72–5, 92, 94–7, 101
complaints 66, 69
compulsory acquisition 63
computerised fire detection 26
computerised information 29
concrete 4
conformity requirements 44, 51
conservation: of fuel/power 72
conservatories 74
consultancy 89
consultants 85–6, 96
consultation: regulations 60; requirements 35, 57–8; threshold 60
Consumer Credit Act 98

contamination: land 83
contractors 17–18, 42, 55, 57–8, 90–2, 94, 96
contractual: arrangements 61, 64; mechanisms 62; obligations 62; protection 68; responsibility 14, 17
controlled fitting: definition 72
controlled service: definition 72
conveyancers 98–101, 105
conveyancing 51, 98–9, 101; responsibilities 99
cooking 112
cooling-off period 98
cooperation/coordination (art 22 FSO) 28
corridors 17–18, 50
councils 7, 29, 41, 68–9, 83
counter-notices 56
court judgments 56, 61
covenant for quiet enjoyment 55, 69
Covid-19 pandemic 8
criminal liability 33
criminal offences 26, 32, 73, 75, 110
crumb foam 111
cupboards 17–8
currency 93
cushions 111

Daejan Investments Ltd v Benson 58
damages 69, 91
damp 112
danger areas: procedures for (art 15 FSO) 24
dangerous substances (arts 12, 16 FSO) 21–3, 25
data 90, 96
databases 93
dealer-arranged finance 98
debt 1, 62, 94
decking 4
decoration 81
deeds 17
defective: cladding 1–2, 6–7, 56–7, 67, 69, 87–97, 108; materials 5; premises 67–70, 83; work 67–8, 73
Defective Premises Act (DPA) 67–70
defects 2, 4, 6, 50, 68, 83, 94, 110
demographic composition 39
deposits, tenancy 107
design errors 4
discretion 17
dispensations 58, 60
disputes (arts 35–36 FSO) 34
disrepair 55–6

domestic premises 17, 26–7, 32, 39, 108, 111; definition 108
doors 3, 10, 13, 17, 24, 39, 41, 50, 54, 72, 80–1; replacement 50
drainage 52, 72, 112
drains 75, 108
due diligence 7, 33, 90–1, 93–5, 98–9, 105

eaves 5
Economic Actor Schedule 93
economic loss 70
electric circuits 72
electrical: appliances 109; fault 9; installations 80, 110; safety *see* electrical safety; work 72
electrical safety 72, 107, 110; certificates 110
electricity 6, 52, 108
electronic format 11, 38–9
electrostatic discharges 19, 22
elevations 4, 9, 47, 104
eligibility criteria 50, 90, 94–5
e-mail 36
Emergencies and escalation of works 60
emergency 9, 11, 16, 21–5, 37, 39, 41, 58, 100; arrangements 25; doors 24; escape 100; evacuation 11, 37, 41; exits 24; lighting 24; measures 23, 25; medical treatment 24; plan 21; routes and exits (art 14 FSO) 24; services 9, 24–5; shutdown 22; works 58
emotional loss 5
employees 15–16, 18–21, 26–8, 32–3, 35, 41; at work, general duties of (art 23 FSO) 28; duty to consult (art 41 FSO) 35; not to be charged for things done or provided under (art 40 FSO) 35; provision of information to (art 19 FSO) 26–7
employers 14–16, 18, 27–8, 33, 35, 95, 109; provision of information to (art 20 FSO) 27
employment 19, 27
energy 22; efficiency 98, 107; performance 98, 107; performance certificate (EPC) 98, 107
enforcement: action 17, 34, 56, 93; agencies 89; authority 36, 111; notice 30–2, 34; powers 93
enfranchisement 63–4
engagement 45, 66, 89
engineering 41, 103
engineers 42, 44, 85, 101, 103

English language 12
enjoyment, quiet 55, 69
enlargement of buildings 67
enquiries 29, 37, 99–100
entrances 39; doors 13; lobbies 17–18, 52
envelope of buildings 79
environment 21, 103; legislation 16
equal rights *see* voting rights
equipment 10, 12, 15, 22–5, 27, 30, 34, 37–8, 60, 82; *see also* firefighting equipment
equity *see* negative equity
escape: means of 77; routes 59, 77; staircase 4
European Classification 80
European Union (EU) 92
evacuation 5, 9, 11–12, 24, 27, 37–9, 41, 77, 82
eviction 55–6
EWS1 form 102–6; disclaimer 102; obtaining and reviewing 104–6
exclusivity 35
excuse 33
exemption 33, 108
exemptions: statutory 18, 63, 87
exit/escape routes 11–12, 24, 59, 77
expenditure 56, 58–9, 91, 99
expertise 103
experts 89, 102
explosions 22, 25, 112
explosive atmospheres 19, 22, 28
explosives 74
exposure to fire 4, 112
extensions 76, 82; residential 20, 72, 74
exterior cladding 9
external cladding systems 1
external fire spread 79–81
external walls: assessors 44–5; construction 40, 42–7; definition 81; fire 88, 100–2; insulation 99; materials 103; survey 103; system (EWS) 1, 3, 93, 101–2
extinguishers, fire 12
extractor fans 10
Eyre, HH Judge, QC 70

fabric 78, 111
façades 9, 42–3, 46–7
facilities: maintenance of (art 38 FSO) 34–5
family 1, 61, 108
fans, extractor 10
farmland 18
fatalities 87

fault 7, 9, 33, 38, 50, 63, 110; fault-based remedies 62
Fellow of the Architecture and Surveying Institute (FASI) 85
Fellow of the Chartered Association of Building Engineers (FCABE) 85
Fellow of the Charters Institute of Building (FCIOB) 85
Fellow of the Institution of Civil Engineers (FICE) 85
Fellow of the Royal Institution of Chartered Surveyors (FRICS) 85
filler materials 103
filling 111
fire: alarm systems 2, 38, 41; damage 5; detection (art 13 FSO) 23–4; detectors 23, 38; doors 3, 8, 10, 12–3, 37, 39, 50, 52, 54; drills 24, 26; exit routes 11; precautions 12, 15, 18; protection 3, 10; remediation works 67; resistant construction 3, 78, 103; risk assessment (FRA) 43–7; stopping 5, 70, 80; suppression systems 78; wardens 26
fire and rescue authorities: definition 29
fire risk appraisal of external wall construction (FRAEW) 43–8
Fire Safety (England) Regulations 2022: summary of 37–9
Fire Safety Act (FSA) 40
fire safety information: definition 82
Fire Safety Order (FSO) 14–40, 43, 47, 50–1, 75–6, 82, 108; alterations notices (art 29) 30–1; appeals (arts 35–36) 34; articles and definitions 16–18; byelaws, suspension of (art 44) 36; civil liability for breach of statutory duty (art 39) 35; cooperation (art 22) 28; coordination (art 22) 28; danger areas, procedures for (art 15) 24; dangerous substances (arts 12, 16) 21–3, 25; disputes (arts 35–36) 34; duties 18–32; duty to consult the enforcing authority before passing plans (art 45) 36; emergency routes and exits (art 14) 24; employees, duty to consult (art 41) 35; employees not to be charged for things done or provided under (art 40) 35; employees at work, general duties of (art 23) 28; employers, provision of information to (art 20) 27; enforcement notices (art 30) 31; facilities, maintenance of (art 38) 34–5; fire detection (art 13) 23–4; Fire Safety (England) Regulations 2022, summary of 37–9; fire safety requirements, enforcement of (arts 25–36) 29–30; firefighters' switches (art 37) 34; firefighting (art 13) 23–4; firefighting equipment, maintenance of (arts 17, 38) 25–6, 34–5; general fire precautions (arts 8, 47) 18–19, 36; Health and Safety of Work Act 36; individual flat owners, ambiguity of position 18; information to employees, provision of (art 19) 26–7; licensed premises, special provisions for (arts 42–43) 35–6; mandatory risk assessments (art 9) 19–20; minimising fire safety risk (arts 10, 11) 20–1; non-applicable premises 18; notices, service of (art 48) 36–7; offences (art 32) 32–3; official guidance (art 50) 37; penalties (art 32) 32–3; prohibition notices (art 31) 31–2; premises (arts 5, 31(10)) 17–18; public authorities, consultation by (art 46) 36; reasonable precautions defence (arts 33–34) 33; regulations about fire precautions, power to make (art 24) 28–9; responsible persons (art 3) 16–17; safety assistance (art 18) 26; self-employed persons, provision of information to (art 20) 27; summary of FSO duties 15–16; training (art 21) 27–8
fire safety requirements: enforcement of (arts 25–36 FSO) 29–30
fire safety risk: minimising (arts 10, 11 FSO) 20–1
firefighters 3–4, 8, 10–2, 34, 38, 45, 81–2; switches (art 37 FSO) 34
firefighting 4, 10–12, 15, 23–5, 38, 60, 82; art 13 FSO 23–4
firefighting equipment: maintenance of (arts 17, 38 FSO) 25–6, 34–5
first aid 24
First Tier Tribunal (FTT) 58, 60–1, 63
fitness for habitation 6; definition 112
flame-fronts 9–10
flammability 29; aluminium 3; cladding 2, 56, 68; reynobond 3; walls 15; wall-cladding 19, 21
floor numbers 12
foam 10, 111
food preparation 112
footprint plans 95
forfeiture 49, 55–6, 61–3
freehold enfranchisement 64

Index 117

freeholders 16, 41, 64, 88
fridge-freezers 9
fuel 9, 72; burning 111; *see also* gas
Fuller Court Blocks, Hornsey 84
fumes 78
funded projects: payment in instalments 92
funding 7, 59, 67, 87–97
furniture 78, 111
Furniture and Furnishings (Fire)(Safety) Regulations 111

garages 108
gardens 108
gas 72–3, 107–10; appliances 109–10; boilers 72; cookers 73; fittings 109; Gas Safe registered engineers 109–10; installations 73; safe 73; safety 72, 107–9; safety certificates 109–10; systems 73
general fire precautions: arts 8, 47 FSO 18–19, 36; definition 18
glass 4, 10, 80; reinforced plastic (GRP) 4–5
glazing 84, 104
government: announcements 7, 87; approved schemes 72, 88; assistance to remove defective cladding 87–97
grants: application 96; dispensation 58, 60; funding 49, 67, 88, 90, 92–6
Greater London Authority (GLA) 89, 92–4
greenhouses 74
Grenfell 1–3, 5–6, 8–14, 28, 37, 39–41, 44, 69, 71, 77, 99; block 3; fire 2–3, 5, 37, 40–1, 71, 77; inquiry 6, 8–13, 28; tower 1, 8, 10–2, 14, 40, 44
ground-landlord 3, 6–7, 14–15, 17, 23, 26, 49–58, 62–3, 68–9, 86, 105
ground-lease 50–1
ground rent 16, 49, 52–3, 55, 62
guarantees 64, 73, 76, 83–4, 88, 102
gutters 108

habitation: fitness for 6, 67–8, 112
hallways 50, 52
Hardie Plank 4
harm 45, 47
harmful substances 22
hazards 3, 22, 24–5, 30, 43, 46, 112; hazardous conditions 19, 22
health and safety 21, 35–6, 59, 71, 82, 84, 103, 109, 112
Health and Safety of Work Act 36
hearings, appeal 34

heat 4, 10, 78, 81–2
heating 108, 110; system 52, 72
higher-risk buildings 7, 28, 63, 65–6, 71, 74, 99
high-rise buildings 2, 8, 11–13, 37, 39, 93, 98–101, 106; definition 37; leaseholders 49; residential 8, 10–1, 13, 37–9, 41, 43, 87–8
high-risk premises 26, 30
high-voltage signs 34
highways, public 100
HMOs (Houses in Multiple Occupation) 107–9, 112; definition 32, 108
HMRC Clearance Team 93
Homes (Fitness for Human Habitation) Act 112
hose reels 12
hostels 80
hot 9, 72, 112; gases 9; objects 112; smoke 9; water 72
hotels 80
house: definition of 18
house-builders 67–8, 83–5, 101
houses in multiple occupation (HMOs) *see* HMOs
housing: Act 32, 61, 93, 107–8; associations 92; authorities 32, 42, 110; communities and 2, 42, 89; estates 76
hovercraft 17
HSE (Health and Safety Executive) 59, 109
human habitation *see* habitation

identity 28, 47
ignitability test 111
ignition sources 19, 22, 79
importers 111
imprisonment 32
incidents 2, 23, 25
indemnity insurance 44, 64, 85, 94, 96
independent: advice 102; arbitrators 61; bodies 29
individual: flat-owners 26, 50, 102, 105; flats 8, 13, 18, 38, 41, 50, 54, 69; leaseholders 1–2, 6, 49, 51, 53–5, 57–8, 64, 90, 99; leases 50, 63–4
industry: association 82; cost 90; knowledge 45; standards 38, 91
inflation 52
information box 11–2, 37–8, 42, 82
ingress 3, 77
injury 1, 5, 32, 35, 67–8
inlets 38

inquest 8
inspections 11, 46, 104
inspectors 29, 75–6, 105
Institution of Fire Engineers (IFE) 103
insulation 3–4, 10, 15, 80, 99, 103; boards 10
insurance 5, 62–4, 85, 94, 96, 99–100; claims 91; companies 51; costs 2; leasehold frameworks 53
insurers 42, 44
internal: alterations 53; arrangements 112; fire 82; fire-spread (structure) 78–9; installation 54; layout 10; linings 78; structure 78; surfaces 52; walls 3, 52
International Monetary Fund (IMF) 93
Internet 42
intumescent materials 80
iron, cast 4
irrecoverable costs 60, 70

James Hardie Building Products Ltd 4
Jenrick, Robert, MP 87
Jervis v Harris clause 55
job-centric checklists 94

keepsakes 5
kitchen fires 9–10, 108–9

LABC (local authority building control) 84
labels 111
laminate balconies 104
Lancashire Combined Fire Authority 29
land: contamination 83; registry 51; use 71
landings 12, 50, 52, 54
landlord responsibilities 50, 107–12; Category Fire Hazards 112; consent 54; costs 56, 68; duties 68, 109; electrical safety certificates 110; function of landlords 64–5; Furniture and Furnishings (Fire) (Safety) Regulations 1988 111; gas safety certificates 109–10; Homes (Fitness for Human Habitation) Act 112; interest 50, 62–4; maintenance and repair responsibilities 108; obligations 55, 62; out-of-pocket expenses 56; relevant documents 107; Smoke and Carbon Monoxide Alarms (England) Regulations 111
language 12, 39, 107
Law Society-recommended forms 99–100
lawful business 15–6
lawful presence at premises 14–5, 23
lease extensions 49
lease terms 51

leasehold: law 17, 56; property 55–6, 59, 99–100; reform 59, 63; service-charges 54, 58, 92, 95; structures 50, 55, 64, 69
leasehold frameworks 49–66; alterations, restrictions on 53; Building Safety Act (2022) 65–6; Building Safety Charge 65–6; commercial premises 65; compliance with regulatory requirements 54; date 51; default provisions 55–7; description of property 52; flats above shops 65; ground rent, amount of 52; insurance 53; landlord obligations 55; leaseholders, collective status as landlords 64–5; personal details 51; repairs, responsibility for 52–3; rights and reservations 52; rules governing behaviour 54–5; sale and subletting, restrictions on 54; service-charge provisions 53; service charges, leaseholder consultation on 57–64; term of lease 51; use of property, restrictions on 54
leaseholders: collective status as landlords 64–5
leases 16, 49–56, 59, 61–4, 69–70, 91–2, 95; terms 49
legislation 6–7, 16, 54, 56, 58, 65, 71, 74, 98, 107, 110; agenda 3; conflict 36; control 47; duplication 33; framework 14; provisions 67; requirements 25, 29, 37; standards 13
lending institutions 51
Levelling Up agenda 42, 89
levies 66, 87; levying of charges 35, 64
liabilities, financial 1, 5, 99
licensed premises: special provisions for (arts 42–43) 35–6
licensing 35
life: risk to 5, 10, 43–4, 46–7, 81, 90
life-safety certificate 102
lifts 11, 17–18, 37–9, 52
lighting 12, 24, 39, 112
lightweight materials 3
linings 78
liquid 112
load-bearing structures 78, 84
loan schemes 7, 88, 102
lobbies 10, 12, 17–18, 39, 50, 52, 54
London Fire Brigade 10
loose filling 111
low lighting 12, 39
lower-rise buildings 43, 87
luminous tube signs 34

magistrates' court 33–4, 36
maintenance and repair: landlord responsibilities 108
maisonettes 38, 53
managing-agent 17, 23, 41–2, 90–1
manual override 22
masonry 3, 43, 80
match test 111
mattresses 111
Member of the Chartered Association of Building Engineers (MCABE) 85
Member of the Chartered Institute of Architectural Technologists (MCIAT) 85
Member of the Chartered Institute of Building (MCIOB) 85
Member of the Institution of Civil Engineers (MICE) 85
Member of the Royal Institution of Chartered Surveyors (MRICS) 85
membranes 5, 80
methodology 42–4
Ministry of Housing, Communities and Local Government (MHCLG) 2, 89–97
money laundering 98
monuments 74
Moore-Bick, Sir Martin 8
mortgages 1, 62, 86, 101, 104; debt 1, 62; instructions 86; lenders 101; liabilities 1; unmortgageable properties 1, 51; unsecured debt 1
multi-occupied buildings 2–3, 5–6, 14–8, 40–1, 45, 50, 54, 99, 101, 104, 107
multi-storey apartments 3, 45
Murphy v Brentwood 70

naked flames 55
narrative accounts 8
National Fire Chief Council: Guidance on Simultaneous Evacuation 41
National House Building Council (NHBC) 68, 83–5
natural lighting 112
natural timber 4
negative equity 1
negligence 35, 98
negotiations 5, 96
neighbouring buildings 79
New Providence Wharf 2
new-build properties 83, 98
no-fault right to manage 63, 65
nominal payments 52–3
nominated persons 27–8, 33, 63, 95
non-accredited companies 26

non-ACM cladding systems 88
non-automatic firefighting equipment 23
non-combustible materials 4
non-compliance 58, 60, 62, 107
non-domestic premises 17, 41; definition 17
non-eligible works 91
non-structural services 3, 52
not-for-profit organisations 16
notices 28, 30–1, 36, 56; prohibition (art 31 FSO) 31–2; service of (art 48 FSO) 36–7
notifications 75
nuclear facilities 74

occupational leases 69–70
offences 26, 73, 75, 110; art 32 FSO 32–3; guilty offenders 33
official advice 77, 104; art 50 FSO 37; guidance 6, 37, 40, 78–9, 106; notices 28, 36–7; statements 98; websites 40
off-site premises 110
operational condition 22, 39, 50, 91
opinions 30–1, 46, 94, 108
organisations 41, 93
outhouses 108
outlets 38
out-of-pocket expenditure 56
owner: definition of 16–17; owner-occupied premises 92

partitions 52, 78
PAS 9980:2022 Fire Risk Appraisal 40–8; Code of Practice 42–8; PEEPS 41–2; purpose-built blocks of flats 41
patrolling 23
penalties (art 32 FSO) 32–3
personal emergency evacuation plans (PEEPs) 11–2, 37, 41–2
pets 54
phenolic foam insulation 10
photographs 5, 47; as evidence 46, 105
pillows 111
pipes 3, 108
plant rooms 74, 80
plasterboard 3–4
plastic 4–5
plumbing 72
polyethylene 3, 9
polyisocyanurate (PIR) 10
polythene 4
porches 74
post-dispute arbitration agreements 61

Index

precautions: defence 33; fire 18–9, 21, 27–8, 30, 33, 36
pre-contract inquiries 98–9
Premier Guarantee 84
premises: arts 5, 31(10) FSO 17–18
Prescribed Hazard: definition 112
pre-tender support 90–2, 95
private landlords *see* landlord responsibilities
Probyn Miers Report 3
procurement strategies 89, 91, 96
pro-forma 86, 99
prohibition notices (art 31 FSO) 31–2
Project Management Office (PMO) 90
property, restrictions on use of 54
proportionality 43, 46
prosecution 33
public authorities: consultation by (art 46 FSO) 36
public-sector bodies 57, 59
purpose-built blocks of flats 41, 51

qualifications 85, 96
qualifying: expenditure 91; items 91; leaseholders 63; leases 64; long-term 57–8;
works 57–8, 91
quantity of materials/substances 22–3, 25, 47
quotations 57–9, 96

rack rent 16
radiators 72
rainscreen 3, 9–10
rating regulations 4, 43, 47, 112
reasonable: costs 53, 91; notice 55; period 4, 78; precautions 33; precautions defence (arts 33–34 FSO) 33; standard 57, 103; steps 27–8, 30, 64, 66, 86, 91, 110
reasonableness test 33, 57, 59, 90
re-entry rights 61
referral 34, 61, 89
refurbishment 1, 8, 12
refuse disposal chutes 52
Registered Providers of Social Housing (RPs) 93
registration 7, 66, 85, 88–90, 92–3; compliance with 54
reimbursement 54, 56
relevant building: definition 80
remedial: action 25, 48, 110; responsibilities 6; works 49, 88, 93, 103–4, 110

remediation 2, 7, 45, 48, 50–1, 64, 86, 88–95
remedies 49–50, 62
re-mortgaging 74
renovation 72
rent 16–17, 52, 56, 65, 107–9; arrears 56; demands 65; *see also* ground rent; rack rent
repairs 25, 52, 55–6, 81; responsibility for 52–3
repossession 56, 62
re-roofing 74
re-sale 51
research and analysis 2
reservations 52
residential ground-lease: concept of 51
Residential Property Developer Tax (RPDT) 7, 87
residential property development activities 87
resistance, fire 4, 29
resources, scarcity of 43–4
responsible persons (art 3 FSO) 16–17; definition 17
restrictions 53–4; on alterations 53; on sale 54
retail 111
re-upholstering 111
revolving doors 24
Reynobond 3
Richmond House fire 3–5
rights 50, 65, 69, 93, 95, 107; and reservations 52
right-to-manage 88
risk: appraisal 40, 42–3; assessment 2, 15, 18–21, 23, 25, 28, 30, 43, 99–100, 103; factors 43, 46–7; mandatory assessment (art 9 FSO) 19–20; proportionate approach 44; rating 43, 47
rolling-stock 18
roofs 5, 9, 50, 55, 64, 68, 72, 79–81, 84
routine safety checks 37–8, 42, 99
Royal Institute of British Architects (RIBA) 85
Royal Institution of Chartered Surveyors (RICS) 58–9, 85, 95, 102, 104
rubbish 55
rules governing behaviour 54–5

safety assistance (art 18 FSO) 26
sale and subletting, restrictions on 54
sale-of-goods legislation 98
sanitary conveniences 108, 112
sanitation 72, 108

scaffolding 91
scheme operators 74–5
scissor-section flats 38
Scotland 13
sealants 80
seals 80
search-and-rescue operations 8, 11–12
Secretary of State 28–9, 31, 34, 37, 57, 59, 63
self-certification 74, 93–5
self-employed persons 15, 27: provision of information to (art 20 FSO) 27
self-evacuation 11, 41–2
service-charges 54, 56–9, 61–2, 64, 67, 88, 92, 107; leaseholder consultation on 57–64; provisions 53
Services of Public Economic Interest (SPEI) 92–3
sewerage 75
sheathing 96
sheltered housing 45
ships 18
shops: flats above 65
showrooms 98
sign-off 95, 97
single households 14, 18, 32, 54, 108
sinks 108
slate 5
smoke: alarms 109, 111; control 38; hoods 12; logging 10; ventilation 31
Smoke and Carbon Monoxide Alarms (England) Regulations 111
snagging 93
social landlords 59, 87, 93
solar panels 81
solicitors 98
solvency 83
sounders 11
Special Drawing Rights (SDR) 93
specified attachment: definition 81
SportCity v Countryside Properties (UK) Ltd 68–70
sprinkler systems 12, 31, 38
stairways 4, 12, 17–18, 39, 52
stake-holders 44, 101
State Aid rules 92
steel 4
stripping-out cladding 57
stud walls 3
subletting 54
subsidies 92
summary conviction 33
Sunak, Rishi, MP 87
sunlight 81

surveyors 42, 59, 77, 85, 95, 102
surveys 10, 46–7, 103, 105
switches 34

taxation 7, 87
technology 21, 27, 73
television 54
tenancy 17, 61, 59, 68, 107–12
terminology 44
thermal 3, 72, 79–80; break 80; bridging 80; elements 72; insulation 3; radiation 79
third-party: accreditation 26, 41; funds 64; management 51
timber 3–5, 73, 104; battens 4–5; buildings 73, 104; burn 4; frame 4; structure 4; stud 3
time-barred construction 67, 70
title-indemnity insurance 51
tort law 69–70
toxic gases 12–3
Trade and Cooperation Agreements (TCAs) 92
training (art 21 FSO) 27–8
transport of dangerous substances 19, 22
trays, cavity 80
trespass 53
triple-glazing 84
Trustpilot 5
tube signs 34

UK Finance Lenders' Handbook 51, 85–6, 101
UK-EU Trade and Cooperation Agreement (TCA) 92
underleases 69
underwriting 83
undue fire 79
unfair competition 92
unfair practices 56
unitary authorities 29
United Kingdom (UK) 92–3
unoccupied flats 61
unsafe cladding 13, 23, 87–9, 91, 97
unsaleable properties 1
upholstery 111
up-to-date plans 11, 51, 101
uPVC 9
urban development 59, 63
utility services 50, 52

value-for-money 59
valuers 42, 101–2, 104
vandalism 37

vapours 112
VAT (Value Added Tax) 93
vehicles 17
ventilation 22, 31, 72, 82, 112
verification 46
vessels 17
victims 1
virtual-freehold 51
visitors 15
voluntary referral 34
volunteers 27
voting rights 65

waking watch 2, 23
walls 1, 3–5, 10, 15, 40, 42–7, 72, 78, 80–1, 88, 93, 99–105; appraisals 42; assessment 43; assessors 44–5; build-ups 45, 47; cladding 14, 19, 21; construction 3, 40, 42–7, 105; double-wall construction 3; exterior 51; fire 88, 100–2; flammability 15; glazing 104; insulation 4, 15, 99; lines 4–5; materials 103; mineral insulation 4; survey 103; system 1, 3, 93, 101–2; types 105; void 5; *see also* external walls

warnings 18, 25; means of 77; systems 26
warranties 83–6, 91, 96, 98; agreement 83; benefits 85; protection 84; providers 7, 84
waste 19, 22, 72, 112
water 3–4, 52, 72, 108, 112; drainage 52; efficiency 72; ingress 3; safety 72; supply 112
waterproofing 5, 80
wayfinder signage 38
wear-and-tear 77
websites 15, 40
well-being 41
well-drawn-up leases 52, 54–5, 68
wet and dry mains 38
wheelchair users 42
windows 8, 10, 17, 72, 81, 84; frames 80; jamb 9; openings 79; replacement 72, 74; surrounds 10
workmanlike manner 67–8, 71, 80
workmanship 47, 80
workplaces 16–18, 41, 76
works contracts 92, 96

yards 108
young people 5, 19; *seealso* children